Spanish:

Learn Spanish for Beginners in a Fun and Easy Way

Including Pronunciation, Spanish Grammar, Reading, and Writing, Plus Short Stories

By: University of Linguistics

Table of Contents

Introduction	5
Chapter 1: How to Learn a New Language	7
The Advantage of Learning as an Adult	7
Main Differences Between English and Spanish	8
Chapter 2: The Fundamentals of Spanish	10
Male-Female Agreement	10
Verb Conjugation	11
Adjectives in Singular and Plural	11
Sentences Without Subject	12
Chapter 3: Basic Spanish Words and Phrases	13
Greetings	13
Introductions	14
Common Expressions and Questions	15
Chapter 4: The Alphabet	17
The Spanish Character Set	17
Pronunciation Differences	18
Chapter 5: Pronunciation	20
Diphthongs & Triphthongs	20
Consonant Sounds	21
Chapter 6: Syllabication	23
Syllabication Structure	24
Chapter 7: Stress and Accents	26
Accent Types	26
Uses of the Tilde	27
Chapter 8: The Use of Numbers, Colors, Time and Feelings	29
Counting in Spanish	29
Describing With Colors	32
Telling the Time	34
Expressing Feelings	36
Chapter 9: Nouns, Articles, and Adjectives	38

Adjectives	38
Articles	39
Nouns	40
Chapter 10: Plurals	**42**
Word Ending in a Vowel	42
Words Ending in Consonants	43
Nouns With Two or More Words and Proper Nouns	44
Chapter 11: Pronouns	**46**
Personal Pronouns	46
Possessive Pronouns	47
Demonstrative Pronouns	48
Chapter 12: Verbs	**50**
Regular Verbs	50
Irregular Verbs	52
Chapter 13: Ser and Estar	**54**
Ser — "to be"	54
Estar — "to be"	55
Chapter 14: Question Formation	**58**
Yes-or-No Questions	58
Open-Ended Questions	59
Chapter 15: Adverbs, Prepositions, and Conjunctions	**62**
Adverbs	62
Prepositions	63
Conjunctions	66
Chapter 16: Forming Sentences	**69**
Sentences Without Subject	69
Negative Sentences	70
Time Expressions	71
Chapter 17: The Imperative and Subjunctive Moods	**73**
Indicative Mood	73
Subjunctive Mood	73
Imperative Mood	75

Chapter 18: Making Comparisons — **78**

Comparative Form — 78

Similarity — 78

Superlative Form — 79

Comparison of Verbs — 80

Chapter 19: Short Stories — **81**

Story #1: Un nuevo empleo / A New Job — 83

Story #2: Como hacer nuevos amigos / How to Make New Friends — 86

Story #3: Mi deporte favorito / My Favorite Sport — 89

Story #4: Comer en un restaurante / Eating in a Restaurant — 92

Story #5: De compras en el centro comercial / Shopping at the Mall — 95

Conclusion 98

Introduction

Welcome to *"Learn Spanish for Beginners in a Fun and Easy Way: Including Pronunciation, Spanish Grammar, Reading, and Writing, Plus Short Stories."* In this book, we are going to jump right into the fundamentals of learning Spanish and how you can maximize your efforts.

If you are reading this, it is because you are keen on learning Spanish in the best possible way. This means that you are looking for the simplest and most effective way to learn one of the world's most important languages.

Of course, you could always sign up for a Spanish school in your city. Or, you could make an adventure out of it and travel to any one of the exotic countries in Latin America. You could even hire a private tutor to work with you on a one-on-one basis.

But let's face the fact that not everyone has the time to dedicate a fixed amount of their time to Spanish lessons. In fact, you might be so busy that just reading this requires you to clear up your schedule. That is why this guide has been designed to get your Spanish skills off the ground quickly and easily.

If you have tried to learn Spanish or another language the old-fashioned way, you can understand where this is coming from. It's not easy to take time out of your already packed schedule to go to class or work with a private tutor. Also, traveling to another country, while exciting, can take a good chunk out of your time, and it doesn't come cheap.

This guide will get you acquainted with the fundamentals of Spanish. You might be surprised to find that it is much easier to learn Spanish than you have initially thought. If you have struggled with it in the past, it is because you haven't found the right approach. That is the goal of this book. It is intended for those who want to maximize their efforts and talents.

In addition, Spanish is used by close to a billion native speakers and about another billion people as a second or third language, making it one of the most prominent languages in the West. As proof, it is among the six of United Nation's official languages.

Beyond that, learning Spanish will open doors to you into a world of culture, literature, and entertainment. Additionally, Latin America is a host to some of the most beautiful countries in the world. As such, these make great travel destinations at a surprisingly affordable price (when compared to traveling to Europe or Asia).

It is not hard to make a compelling case when it comes to the importance of learning Spanish. There are countless reasons that learning Spanish will improve your overall skillset even if you don't need it for work. Speaking multiple languages not only opens doors to other cultures but also has health benefits, such as improved cognition and concentration. Learning a second or third language has been linked to improved memory skills and heightened learning skills.

Plus, learning new languages can become one of those hobbies that just snowballs over time.

Why not?

If you have been thinking about taking up languages as a hobby or simply as a new challenge, then look no further. This guide, in addition to subsequent guides, will help you get on the road (and stay on it) to mastering a new language. You will feel satisfied with yourself and your accomplishments after you learn Spanish through this guide. The longer you wait, the more you are missing out on this wonderful experience.

Chapter 1: How to Learn a New Language

For most folks, learning a new language is one of the most challenging things they will ever do in their lives. The reason for this is that languages don't come easy. They take time and dedication for the learner to achieve a certain level of proficiency.

It takes several years of study and development before we can be reasonably proficient in a language. It is around the age of 7 or 8 when a child is able to communicate fairly well. Nevertheless, it takes a few more years of schooling and training before an individual truly masters a language. Even then, some folks are unable to go beyond a certain level of mastery.

The Advantage of Learning as an Adult

The big difference between learning a language as a child and learning a language as an adult lies in the fact that many of the cognitive processes, which children need to develop, have already been developed.

What does that mean?

It means that you don't need to go back and re-learn the alphabet or work on phonics. You can begin to reasonably decode a new language with some helpful pointers. Also, this means that you don't have to learn the mechanics of reading and writing. These are skills that you have already gotten a handle on in your native language.

So, what happens when you learn a new language is that you are transferring the skills you have already developed in your native language to the new language that you are learning. While that sounds rather straightforward, there are some bumps along the way.

First of all, language systems tend to vary significantly.

In general, languages function like complex systems that depend on logic. Every language has its own logic. However, that logic doesn't always make sense when compared to other languages. In fact, when you look at language, it is like getting a glimpse into the way the mind of people works.

Secondly, some languages share a common ancestry, while others have no relation between them, whatsoever. Most Indo-European languages share some kind of similarity among them. This can be observed in the syntax (word order) and the structure of words themselves. If this is the case, then it is a lot easier to make sense of the way such a language is structured.

Thirdly, some languages share a common base from which they splinter off into different directions. One such example is the so-called "romance languages." These languages share a common ancestry in the Latin spoken by the old Roman Empire. That common base can be seen in the syntax and similarity in roots and word families. Yet, the similarities pretty much end there. Each language (Spanish, French, Italian, and so on) go off into their own direction, thus making them unique in their own right.

Main Differences Between English and Spanish

So, what can you do to make learning a new language easier on you?

Based on the previous examples, the first aspect to consider is syntax. In the case of English and Spanish, they both share common syntax insofar as the subject preceding the verb. Then, the object of the verb follows right after the verb. This basic structure is essentially the same. However, there are some subtle differences. For instance, adjectives precede nouns in Spanish, whereas the opposite is true in English.

Also, romance languages make use of gender-specific nouns. This is one of the most significant differences between English and Spanish. For example, Spanish has a specific gender assigned to all nouns in the language. Now, determining the gender for each noun depends on its spelling. A general rule of thumb, in this case, is that "o" ending nouns are treated as masculine nouns, while the feminine nouns are identified with "a" ending nouns. This is a general rule of thumb, and there are a number of exceptions. Nevertheless, it is a good standard to rely on.

There is also a far more complex verb conjugation system in Spanish than in English. The most complex verb conjugations in English can be found with irregular verbs in the past tense and the past participle form. Beyond that, verb conjugation is fairly self-explanatory in English.

In Spanish, though, verb conjugations are dependent on verb tense and the verb ending of the verb in its infinitive form. This difference can make conjugating verbs seem hard. But once you become familiar with the patterns for each type of verb, you will find it to be much easier than you had initially anticipated.

These three main differences make English rather different from Spanish and are the source of frustration for many Spanish learners. In this guide, we will not only focus on these differences but also on other insider tips that will surely help you gain an advantage in your endeavors with the Spanish language.

Now, here are some general guidelines that you can follow when learning Spanish.

- Listening practice is one of the most important exercises you can do on a regular basis. There are many audiovisual materials online. These materials will help you train your ear for the sound or the "music" of the Spanish language. In this case, you will not only hone your listening skills but also your pronunciation skills.
- Vocabulary lists are old-fashioned but still hold their merits. Now, we are not advocating that you make long lists of words and pound them into your mind. What we are saying is keep a journal of the language you learn on a daily basis. This journal can be something as simple as writing down new words and expressions you learn. You can use drawings, pictures, and notes to help you imprint their meanings in your mind.
- Grammar rules can be effective if that is something that you find useful. Not all people find grammar rules to be particularly useful and engaging. So, if you feel that writing out rules will help you fixate meaning in your mind, then, by all means, do so. If you don't feel too keen on memorizing rules, schematics, such as

- flowcharts and diagrams, can certainly help you gain a much different visual perspective.
- The use of translation is alright at the beginning. While you will hear some teachers say that translation will actually harm your development, it is worth mentioning that translation can help you navigate through the meaning of words and grammar in the very early stages of your development. Later on, translation can help you when you are traveling or interacting with other folks who may require your assistance.
- Watching movies and TV shows are a great source of language for you to learn. Also, music is a wonderful way to become close to the Spanish language. So, take a shot learning a song you like, or simply enjoying a telenovela. You will find that exposing yourself to Latin American culture from the get-go will pay off right away.

In the next chapter, we are going to take a look at the fundamental underpinnings of the Spanish language and how you can get a grip on the most important secrets to gain proficiency as a new Spanish speaker.

Chapter 2: The Fundamentals of Spanish

Spanish, like all languages, has its own nuances that make it truly unique. And while it shares common ancestry with French and Italian, Spanish does have its own characteristics, which can make it tricky for English speakers to master.

The great thing about learning languages nowadays is that we have been able to get to the root of how language systems work. This implies that you don't have to guess as to how a language works. That work has already been done for you. The endeavors of great linguists have led to a deep understanding of how languages work and how they can be learned.

That translates into a flattening of the curve for learners such as you. In the past, most language learners either needed to drill down and figure out how a language worked by themselves or just "go with the flow." The problem with either approach is that it doesn't allow you to gain a full appreciation of the way you can learn a language in an efficient manner.

That being said, Spanish is a rather straightforward language to learn. While it does have its intricacies, these are not as complex as you might think. As such, we will go over them in order to lay sound ground rules that can help you get your Spanish skills off the ground.

So, let us explore the fundamentals rules of the language and how they can be compared to the way English works. In this manner, you will be able to focus on the most troublesome areas that English speakers have when learning Spanish.

Male-Female Agreement

The first thing that jumps out at English speakers is the use of the male-female agreement. This characteristic of Spanish is quite different from English, considering the fact that English is a gender-neutral language. As such, getting used to the male-female agreement is a bit challenging early on.

The main rule of thumb for the male-female agreement is based on observing the spelling of the noun in question. Initially, the article attached to the noun will be your first clue. So, if the article preceding a noun is "el," then it's masculine. It the article preceding the noun is "la," then it is feminine.

However, what happens if you do have the article? Then you must rely on the spelling of the word. As we have mentioned before, "-o" ending nouns are masculine, and "-a" ending nouns are must be treated as feminine. For example, "toro" (bull) is masculine. So, you would express it as "el toro" (the bull). In the case of "vaca" (cow), it is considered feminine. So, you would express it as "la vaca" (the cow).

These examples make a clear point of how you can use the "o" and "a" rule to give you a heads up on the gender of a noun.

Verb Conjugation

Another important rule to consider in Spanish is verb conjugation. Now, conjugation may seem a bit tricky, but it is not quite as tough as it seems.

The foundation for verb conjugation depends on the ending of the infinitive form of the verb. There are three types of endings for the infinitive form of verbs: AR, ER, and IR.

Based on these endings, you will find that they can be conjugated in either the past, present, or future forms. Here are some examples of verbs in the infinitive form based on their endings:

Verbs ending in "AR" are as follows:

- Jugar (to play)
- Saltar (to jump)
- Cantar (to sing)
- Volar (to fly)
- Mirar (to look)

Verbs ending in "ER" are as follows:

- Comer (to eat)
- Volver (to return)
- Aprender (to learn)
- Entender (to understand)
- Acceder (to access)

"IR" ending verbs:

- Sentir (to feel)
- Transmitir (to transmit)
- Abrir (to open)
- Corregir (to correct)
- Permitir (to permit)

As you can see, all Spanish verbs in their infinitive form will all fall into one of these three groups. Later on, we will discuss verb conjugation in depth. We have an entire chapter devoted to verb conjugation. In this chapter, you will see how straightforward verb conjugation can be in Spanish.

Adjectives in Singular and Plural

Another potentially complex aspect of Spanish grammar is the singular and plural form of adjectives. The general rule in English is that adjectives do not have a plural form. In Spanish, adjectives not only agree in terms of male and female but also singular and plural.

A great example of this form can be seen in colors. Colors must agree in terms of both color and quantity. Let's use "azul" (blue) as an example. So, "ojos azules" (blue eyes) agree both in terms of gender ("ojos" is male) and number ("azules" is plural). This exemplifies how it is important to make sure that adjectives agree with the subject of the sentence, both in terms of gender and number.

On the subject of nouns and adjectives, in English, adjectives precede nouns. In Spanish, it is the opposite. For instance, "zapatos negros" (black shoes) agrees both in terms of

gender and number. But you can also see how the noun comes before the color. This is an important difference, but it's an easy one to remember, as it is just essentially the opposite of the word order used in English.

Sentences Without Subject

One other important nuance of Spanish that is shared among the romance languages is that the subject of the sentence isn't always needed. What that means is that the subject of the verb can be omitted in cases where it is absolutely clear what the subject is or if it can be inferred what the subject is.

Let's consider this example: "soy de Inglaterra" (I am from England). Notice that the subject "yo" (I) is not included as the verb "soy" (am), which makes it perfectly clear that you are referring to yourself. As such, the subject can be omitted since it can be easily inferred whom you are talking about. In those cases, when there are references to multiple people and objects, omitting the subject can lead to confusion. Consequently, you might have to ask for clarification or even offer it in order to make sure no information gets lost along the way.

In the following chapters, we will be taking a look at these and other equally important aspects of Spanish at great length. So, buckle up because we are going for quite a ride.

Chapter 3: Basic Spanish Words and Phrases

When starting out with Spanish, you definitely need to get some basic words and phrases so that you can communicate with the people you meet and interact with in common social settings, such as restaurants, airports, bars, or any other places.

That is why we are going to take a look at some words and phrases that you can use right out of the box. Most importantly, they will be able to help you make the most of your social interactions when you travel or find yourself in a group of Spanish speakers. Moreover, these expressions can also help you when you find yourself in a business context with Spanish speakers.

Greetings

First of all, greetings are essential. Consider these:

- Buenos días (good morning)
- Buenas tardes (good afternoon)
- Buenas noches (goodnight / good evening)

There are three simple greetings that you can use to greet other folks when you see them. The rule of thumb is that any time before noon is considered to be "buenos días." Starting at noon, the greeting switches to "buenas tardes." Then, as soon as it gets dark, the greeting switches to "buenas noches."

Also, notice that there is no "good evening" in Spanish. That is why any time it is dark, you would use the "buenas noches" greeting. We will be covering this particular point in greater depth in the chapter regarding time.

It should also be noted that when you are greeting people after midnight, "buenas noches" applies if you still have not gone to bed. However, if you are getting up very early in the morning, then the greeting switches to "buenos días" since you are starting out your day.

For instance, if you are returning from a party at two o'clock in the morning, your greeting would be buenas noches as you still haven't gone to bed. By the same token, if you are rising at two o'clock in the morning, that is, your day is starting out, then you may greet folks as "buenos días."

When greeting people, the traditional "hola" (hello) can't go wrong. This is a universal way in which you can greet people in Spanish. It can be used in both formal and informal contexts. You can combine it as "hola, buenos días" (hello, good morning), and you instantly have the means to approach anyone, especially strangers, in public settings.

Here are some expressions which you can use to ask people how they are doing:

- ¿Qué haces? (What are you doing?)
- ¿Cómo está usted? (How are you?) – formal
- ¿Qué pasa? (What's happening?)
- ¿Cómo estás? (How are you?) – informal
- ¿Qué tal? (What's up?)

- ¿Qué onda? (What's up?) – very informal

These expressions are all variations of "how are you?" though the difference lies in the level of formality, which they represent.

Also, you can use the following expressions to respond to these greetings.

- Bien, gracias. (Good, thank you)
- Muy bien. (Very well)
- Más o menos. (so-so)

These responses are all typical and can be used in any situation. If you happen to be feeling unwell, you could use an expression, such as "no me siento bien" (I feel unwell), especially if you are being asked by the medical staff.

You can follow greetings with:

- ¿Y usted? (and you?) – formal
- ¿Y tú? (and you?) – informal

So, you might have a conversation such as this:

- Hola, buenos días. ¿Cómo estás?
    - Bien gracias, ¿y tú?
- Muy bien, gracias.

This brief exchange illustrates how these expressions can be used to greet a person in virtually any type of context.

Introductions

When introducing yourself, you can use the following to indicate your name:

- Mi nombre es _____. (My name is _____.)
- Me llamo _____. (My name is _____.)

Both expressions are used to state your name, though "me llamo" literally means, "I am called." However, the meaning of this phrase is "my name is..."

To ask for a person's name, you can use the following:

- Formal: ¿Cuál es su nombre? (What is your name?)
- Informal: ¿Cómo te llamas? (What is your name?)

Both questions are asking the person to indicate their name, though the latter literally means "what are you called?" Nevertheless, both questions are asking for the person's name. The response could be either "Me llamo..." or "Mi nombre es..."

Another great expression which you can use when introducing yourself is: "soy de..." (I am from...)

For example, you can say, "Soy de una gran ciudad en los Estados Unidos." (I am from a large city in the United States.). All you need to do in this case is insert the name of your country or city so that your interlocutors know where you are from.

Common Expressions and Questions

Here are some more essential Spanish expressions:

- Aquí tiene (here you go)
- De nada (you're welcome)
- Disculpe (excuse me)
- Lo siento (I'm sorry)
- Muchas gracias (Thank you very much)
- Perdón (pardon, though it can also be used as "excuse me")
- Gracias (Thank you)
- Por favor (please)

These expressions will certainly come in handy when you are traveling through airports, going to restaurants, or interacting with folks in public places, such as offices, shops, or hotels. Also, they are universal and polite, and they work well in any Spanish-speaking country.

Now, let's take a look at some questions that can be used in a variety of situations:

- ¿Cuánto cuesta esto? (How much is this?)
- ¿Puede ayudarme? (Can you help me?)
- ¿De dónde eres? (Where are you from?)
- ¿Dónde vives? (Where do you live?)
- ¿Dónde está _____? (Where is _____?)
- ¿Qué hora es? (What time is it?)
- ¿Dónde puedo encontrar un taxi?) (Where can I find a taxi?)
- ¿Puede hablar más despacio? (Can you speak slower?)
- ¿Puedo ayudarle? (Can I help you?)
- ¿Puede repetir, por favor? (Can you repeat, please?)
- ¿Qué significa _____? (What does _____ mean?)

The questions above are all great for socializing and getting to know other folks. Plus, you can use them in virtually any type of social setting, from an informal gathering to a formal business meeting. You can make them more polite by adding "por favor."

Here are some other great expressions that will surely come in handy at any time.

- Claro (of course)
- Estoy perdido (I am lost)
- Hablo poco español (I speak a little Spanish)
- No (no)
- No entiendo (I don't understand)
- No sé (I don't know)
- No tengo idea (I don't have any idea)
- Nunca (never)
- Sí (yes)
- Siempre (always)
- Sin problema (no problem)

- Tal vez (perhaps)

All of these expressions are good for getting around in Spanish-speaking countries. They can help you navigate the situations in which you find yourself.

Now, let's look at some expressions which you can use on various occasions.

- ¡Salud! (cheers)
- Bienvenido (welcome, singular)
- Bienvenidos (welcome, plural)
- Buen provecho (bon appetit)
- Felicitaciones (congratulations)
- Feliz cumpleaños (happy birthday)
- Qué la pase bien (hope you have a good time)

These expressions are used in various social situations. Perhaps the most uncommon expression for English speakers is "buen provecho." This expression is used when sitting down at the table before eating and then again upon leaving the table after a meal. It basically means "have a good meal," and its closest equivalent would be "bon appetite." Don't be surprised if you hear this expression when eating. You can simply reply with "buen provecho" any time you hear it directed at you.

Lastly, let's take a look at some expressions that we can use to say goodbye:

- Adiós (goodbye)
- Hasta luego (see you later)
- Cuídate (take care)
- Hasta mañana (see you tomorrow)
- Buen viaje (have a good trip)
- Tenga buen día (have a nice day, formal)
- Nos vemos (see you, very informal)
- Tenga buena noche (have a good night)

As you can see, these expressions can be used to take your leave. They vary in formality, though you could combine "nos vemos" with a specific time or date at the end of a business meeting. For example, "nos vemos la próxima semana" (see you next week) can be used to indicate that you will have another meeting next week.

By now, you have enough tools to get around Spanish-speaking countries. That way, you will know what to respond in virtually any situation and circumstances. Best of all, you will be both polite and friendly. You can't go wrong with that!

Chapter 4: The Alphabet

The alphabet used in Spanish is exactly the same as the one in English. This is the Latin alphabet and contains no variations when compared to the English character set. This makes it very easy to identify letters and words in Spanish. Pronunciation, however, is a different story.

The Spanish character set contains the same 26 letters used in English, plus an additional character known as "ñ" (pronounced /enyeh/). This is an additional character, which is essentially exclusive to Spanish. The accent atop the "n" is called "vergulilla." It is only used on the "n" to form the "ñ," and it is not used on vowels such as the case of Portuguese.

Recently, the Real Academia Española – RAE - (Royal Spanish Academy) dropped the official recognition of the letters "ch," "rr," and "ll." These double consonants were previously considered to be letters in their own right, given the spelling of some words. However, the RAE deemed them not to be letters. So, the sounds they produce are the result of a consonant combination and not the product of an individual letter.

The Spanish Character Set

First, let us examine the Spanish character set below:

Aa	Bb	Cc	Dd	Ee	Ff
/ah/	/beh/	/seh/	/deh/	/eh/	/efeh/
Gg	Hh	Ii	Jj	Kk	Ll
/heh/	/acheh/	/ee/	/hota/	/kah/	/eleh/
Mm	Nn	Ññ	Oo	Pp	Qq
/emeh/	/eneh/	/enyeh/	/oh/	/peh/	/kooh/
Rr	Ss	Tt	Uu	Vv	Ww
/ereh/	/eseh/	/teh/	/ooh/	/veh/	/doble ooh/
Xx	Yy	Zz			
/ehkees/	/ee greeahguh/	/zehtah/			

Table 1. The Spanish alphabet

The figure above presents the full character set for the Spanish alphabet. As you can see, the only character not present in the English language is the "ñ." The significant variation between the two alphabets lies in the pronunciation of each letter.

Another similarity between English and Spanish is the use of the same designation of characters for vowel sounds. The traditional A, E, I, O, U letters are used to represent vowel sounds. Given the phonetic construction of Spanish, there are only five vowel sounds and a combination of diphthongs and triphthongs. There are also no long nor short sounds like in English. Overall, there are 14 vowel sounds in English as compared to the five basic sounds in Spanish. It should be noted that whenever there is a combination of vowels written together, they must all be pronounced individually. For example, in "día" (day), the "ee-ah" vowels are pronounced together. This is important to keep in mind, especially if you are used to French where multiple vowels combine to form one sound.

As for the consonants, each letter has its own individual sound. When combined, the sound of each letter must be pronounced just as with vowels. There are a couple of exceptions, however.

First, the double "L" combination makes a "y" sound. For instance, "Lluvia" is not pronounced as /lloveeah/ but rather /youveeah/. As mentioned earlier, the "ll" combination was once considered to be an individual letter but has recently been changed by the RAE.

The same goes for the use or "rr." For example, "guardarropa" (wardrobe) would be considered "rr" as an individual letter. Since the RAE no longer recognizes "rr" as a letter, the pronunciation of the word remains the same, but the official spelling of the word is officially "r-r" as opposed to "rr."

One other letter that is no longer recognized by the RAE is "ch." This letter is now the "c-h" combination as opposed to the former "ch."

Now, let's take a look at pronunciation.

Pronunciation Differences

In general, Spanish is a very easy language to read since each letter represents one sound and must be pronounced as such. In other words, Spanish is read and pronounced exactly as it is spelled. This is one clear advantage that Spanish has over other languages.

Nevertheless, there are some phonological differences between English and Spanish.

The first and perhaps the most obvious is the "rolling R." The rolling Rs tend to give native English speakers a hard time. Perhaps the best comparison of this sound can be found in the Irish accent. The rolling R in the Irish accent is actually quite similar to the one in Spanish. Of course, it takes some time and practice. But given time, you, too, can learn to pronounce it appropriately.

Another key difference lies in the pronunciation of "Q." In English, words with "Q," such as "quick," are pronounced as /kwik/. In Spanish though, they are pronounced as /k/. For instance, "queso" (cheese) is not pronounced as /kwehsoh/ but as /kehsoh/.

This is a very significant difference as it can lead to some miscommunication both when listening and speaking. Sure, it may not derail meaning altogether, but it will make it somewhat difficult to get the message across.

Then, there is the matter of the silent "H." This letter is never pronounced in Spanish, though it is used in writing. So, "hotel" would not be /hotel/ but /ohtel/. This is a very straightforward rule. So, please don't pronounce the "h" whenever you see it printed.

The "G" and "J" can be somewhat confusing. They both produce the /h/ sound depending on the vowel combination. Now, "J" is easy as it will always produce the /h/ sound. The difference lies with "G." In the combinations "GE" and "GI," the sound is /heh/ and /hee/. For example, "general" would be pronounced as /hehneral/ and "giro" (turn) would be /heeroh/. In the case of "GA," "GO," and "GU," the soft /g/ sound is produced. For instance, "gato" (cat) would be /gahtoh/, "golf" would be /gohlf/, and "gustar" (like) would be /goostoh/. Please bear these differences in mind when reading through Spanish text and when pronouncing words.

The last point on pronouncing letters lies with "B" and "V." In European Spanish, both letters sound the same as their English counterparts. However, in Latin American Spanish, both letters sound exactly the same; that is, they have the same bilabial /b/ sound. So, "botar" (drop) and "votar" (vote) both sound the same /bohtahr/. Since they are both indistinguishable, it is up to you to recognize the context where the words are used. That will give you enough reference to determine which word is being said.

On the whole, the Spanish alphabet is pretty straightforward. This is certainly an advantage for native speakers of English or any other romance language. Do take the time to go over each letter and its pronunciation. You will soon find that they are not as hard as you might have thought.

Chapter 5: Pronunciation

Spanish pronunciation has its intricacies as all languages do. On the whole, the overall sound of the language is a lot softer when compared to other languages, such as eastern European or Asian languages. What this means is that most of the sounds are articulated in the higher part of the throat.

Also, the tongue plays a vital role in articulating sounds properly. This is especially true in the case of the rolling Rs. For most English speakers, the rolling Rs tend to be quite a bit of a challenge. Nevertheless, with some practice and dedication, clear pronunciation can be achieved.

Another important aspect of Spanish phonetics is that all vowels must be pronounced individually. The only combination of vowels occurs with the "gu" and "qu" combination. For example, "guerra" does not require the "u" to be pronounced as in /gwerra/. Rather, the pronunciation is similar to /gerra/.

Diphthongs & Triphthongs

Now, one of the things that tends to be somewhat tricky early on is the pronunciation of several vowels in a word. When you have two vowel sounds in succession, you are pronouncing a "diphthong." When you have three sounds, this is called a "triphthong."

Diphthongs are quite common in Spanish. For example, the "ía" ending used in the habitual past is pronounced as /ee-ah/. So, words such as "corría" /koh-ree-ah/ (would run) or "comía" /koh-mee-ah/ (would eat) are good examples of diphthongs.

Here are some examples of diphthongs in Spanish:

- Aire
- Automóvil
- bailar
- Oigo
- Prisionero

As you become more and more familiar with the way Spanish is pronounced, you will find that diphthongs are actually quite easy to identify and pronounce. So, do take the time to go over these items.

With regard to triphthongs, these can be a bit tricky, especially since they aren't that common in English. For instance, "hour," "flour," "fire," and "dire" illustrate the way in which you can pronounce three vowel sounds in a single word. "Flour" /flow-ooh-uhr/ has three sounds, though native speakers tend to reduce the overall sound down to two. This can be quite tricky for English learners, as they might have some difficulty pronouncing these sounds. Luckily for them, triphthongs aren't nearly as prevalent in English as they are in Spanish.

Here as some examples of triphthongs in Spanish:

- Bioinformática

- Buey
- Cambiáis
- Semiautomático
- Uruguay

Just like in the case of English, most native Spanish speakers will reduce these sounds in order to suit their accent best. As such, you might not be able to pick up on the individual sounds quite easily at first. Nevertheless, as you gain more practice with them, you will be able to clearly hear the various sounds in action.

Consonant Sounds

As far as consonants go, these tend to be articulated much the same way as English, though they are "softer" than their English counterparts. For example, /t/ does not have the same hard sound, especially at the end of the word. So, "importante" /im-por-tahn-teh/ has a "softer" sound in both "Ts." The hard sounding "T," as well as "R" is a dead giveaway that your first language is English.

Consequently, the best way for you to pick up on the correct pronunciation of Spanish vowels and consonants is to practice listening as much as you can. The best thing about listening is that you can pick up the way native Spanish speakers utter the various consonant sounds.

Now, here's a couple of interesting points about consonant sounds in Spanish.

First, bear in mind that the /v/ and /b/ sounds have no distinction in Latin American accents. While European Spanish speakers do make this differentiation, Latinos won't. So, you might get crossed up with some of the words being spoken. In addition, the /f/ and /v/ sounds, while articulated in English in the same way, are dissimilar in Spanish.

The same goes for the /s/ and /z/ sounds. Both of these sounds are identical in Latin American Spanish. For instance, "zapato" (shoe) would be pronounced with an /s/ sound as in /sapato/ as opposed to the /z/ sound. As an English speaker, you can certainly use the /z/ with any word that contains the letter "z." However, bear in mind that Latinos won't make this distinction.

The letter "z" does prove to be a bit of a curveball in European Spanish. In European Spanish, the /z/ sound is more similar to using the "th" letter combination in English. As such, "zapato" would sound more like /thahpahto/. While there really isn't anything wrong with either pronunciation style, it all boils down to your ability to pick up on these differences when hearing other speakers.

Another consonant combination to keep in mind are the "sh" and "ch" combinations. For instance, "chocolate" would be /choh-koh-lah-the/ (notice how each set of vowels is pronounced). However, the "sh" sound isn't native to Spanish. In fact, the sound exists because it has been imported from other languages. For example, "show" and "flash" have been imported directly from English. This is evident in the fact that a word such as "desahcer" (undo) would be pronounced as /dehs-ah-sehr/ and not /desh-ah-ser/. So, while Spanish speakers do utilize the sound, it is not inherent to the language. Rather, it has been imported from other languages.

At this point, it is worth mentioning that Spanish pronunciation is quite straightforward once you get the hang of the individual sounds that comprise it. While you may struggle somewhat with the various accent variations from country to country, it is worth noting that the more time you spend in a single country, the more familiar you will become with that accent.

Think about it this way. Imagine English learners learning English in Scotland and then moving to Australia.

These differences can be tough at first. Hence, it is recommended that you focus on the accent of the region that you are going to visit. So, if you are planning to travel to Mexico, try your best to become familiar with the Mexican accent. If you are looking to travel to Colombia, then becoming familiar with the Colombian accent is a must. The best part of all is that websites such as YouTube are filled with videos and tutorials on the various Latin American accents.

Here's one final note: you will hear newscasters use a flatter, more neutral accent. This is intended to reduce the amount of confusion that may arise from one regional accent to another. As such, this type of accent is the kind that you can shoot for in order to help yourself be understood everywhere you go.

Chapter 6: Syllabication

Syllabication is the separation of words into smaller units based on the sounds that are produced. In general, a syllable will consist of a vowel and consonant sound. Sometimes, syllables can be individual vowel sounds, though they are never individual consonant sounds.

When looking at the way syllables are formed in all languages, these tend to break down based on the natural phonological patterns of that language. Nevertheless, the vowel-consonant connection is common throughout virtually all languages.

It is generally accepted that early human language was monosyllabic; that is, early human communication was done through the utterance of individual sounds. To this day, we still use monosyllabic communication to convey meaning. For example, expressions such as "huh" can be used to indicate a specific meaning. Other essential words in English, like "yes" and "no" are classic examples of monosyllabic communication.

With the evolution of human language, communication became more and more complex. This led to the union of individual sounds in order to form words. Now, it should be noted that monosyllabic utterances are also words (such as "I"). Nevertheless, these are generally considered to be isolated sounds. This is especially true when these isolated sounds do not actually have any meaning attached to them.

As human communication becomes richer, the need for more and more words led to the use of syllables under various combinations. This is the reason that one of the most effective methods used to teach kids how to read is based on phonics.

Phonics is composed of core sounds; when combined, they can produce a myriad of words. Consequently, phonics, as individual syllables, can be used to make words. At the end of the day, the words that we use in daily conversation are nothing more than the aggregate of any number of syllable combinations.

Spanish is no exception to this evolution. Children in Spanish schools are taught to read and write using these basic building blocks of language. Initially, children learn the five-vowel sounds before moving on to isolated consonant sounds. Then, vowels sounds are tacked on to individual consonant sounds. For example, children are taught to read, "ma," "me," "mi," "mo," "mu." These syllables, in themselves, are meaningless. However, when they are combined with other such combinations, they can lead to word formation.

Let's take a quick look at how these syllables can be used to make words. For instance, "mama" is one of the first words children in Spanish schools begin to read. So, just like children in English schools learn to read English and pronounce it correctly using phonics, children in Spanish schools use these segregated syllables to make their first words.

Syllabication Structure

As such, each consonant is combined with the five vowel sounds to produce words. Let's take a closer look at this syllabication structure:

- Ba, be, bi, bo, bu
- Ca, ce, ci, co, cu
- Da, de, di, do, du
- fa, fe, fi, fo, fu
- ga, ge, gi, go, gu
- ha, he, hi, ho, hu
- ja, je, ji, jo, ju
- ka, ke, ki, ko, ku
- la, le, li, lo, lu
- ma, me, mi, mo, mu
- na, ne, ni, no, un
- ña, ñe, ñi, ño, ñu
- pa, pe, pi, po, pu
- ra, re, ri, ro, ru
- sa, se, si, so, su
- ta, te, ti, to, tu
- va, ve, vi, vo, vu
- wa, we, wi, wo, wu
- ya, ye, yi, yo, yu
- za, ze, zi, zo, zu

The two letters that are excluded from this list are "Q," as it is always combined with "U" and produce a /k/ sound, and "X" which is not used at the beginning of words. In fact, there are a few exceptions, such as "xilófono" (xylophone), where it is used at the beginning of a word.

From here onward, you can combine any number of these syllables to make your own words. Consider this:

- ma + pa = mapa (map)
- ro + sa = rosa (rose)
- ta + za = taza (cup)
- ca + ma = cama (bed)
- tu + yo = tuyo (yours)

These are two-syllable words. And then here are some three-syllable words:

- to + ma + te = tomate (tomato)
- pa + ta + ta = patata (potato)
- ta + ja + da = tajada (slice)
- pa + pa + ya = papaya (papaya)
- ba + ti + do = batido (smoothie)

As you can see, Spanish is built on these individual syllable combinations. As you become more familiar with the language, you will see that all words can be broken down into these consonant-syllable units. This will make reading far easier while helping you get a grip on the proper pronunciation of the words.

The best way to go about your understanding of syllabication in Spanish is to repeat the various consonant-vowel combinations until you are able to begin forming your own words. At first, you'll have a list of two-syllable words. Then, you will begin to recognize three-syllable words, then four, and so on.

A word of caution: by now, you may have noticed that some words have an accent on them. As such, it is important to note that an accent indicates that the syllable is to be stressed. If there is no accent used in a word, then you will have to listen to the way it is pronounced.

Later on, we will be taking an in-depth look into the way accents are used in Spanish. But for now, it is important to be on the lookout for these accents. These will give you a clear indication as to how a word is pronounced.

And if you are ever in doubt with regard to the pronunciation of a word, tools such as spanishdict.com and Wordreference will help you get the right pronunciation. Best of all, you will be able to hear the way a word is pronounced in various Spanish accents. This is certainly an educational tool that will help you get it right every single time.

Chapter 7: Stress and Accents

In the previous chapter, we focused on syllabication of Spanish words. In that chapter, we mentioned the use of accents in Spanish as a means of indicating word stress.

But before we move on to the use of accents, let's establish what we mean by "stress." Stress refers to the syllable where a word receives its inflection. This inflection is what makes the word sound logical in a given language.

Consider this example:

The word, "chocolate" in English would be pronounced as CHOcolate. In this case, notice how the first syllable receives the stress. The same word, "chocolate" in Spanish, would be pronounced as chocoLAte. Please notice how the third syllable is the one that receives the stress. This is why you often hear Spanish speakers stress words incorrectly in English. While this won't necessarily hinder communication, it may lead to misunderstandings at some point.

Now that we have defined what stress is, there are some ground rules to the use of accents in Spanish.

Accent Types

First, there are three accent types. The first is known as "tilde." The tilde is used exclusively on vowels. It can be used to indicate that the syllable is to be stressed. For example, "comunicación" (communication) ought to be pronounced as comunicaCIÓN. Hence, the stress is placed on the last syllable.

Next, the other type of accent used on vowels is called a "diérisis" (dieresis). This accent mark is used exclusively in the "gu" combination. It is a bit of a rarity in Spanish, but it is present in some very common words. For example, "pingüino" (penguin) and "bilingüe" (bilingual) use this accent mark.

The reason for the use of the dieresis lies in the fact that the "gu" combination with other vowels produces a hard sound. For instance, "guerra" (war) is pronounced as /geh-rah/. However, if the dieresis is used as "güerra," then you would have a soft sound like /gweh-rah/. Needless to say, "güerra" does not exist in Spanish. Nevertheless, the use of the accent makes all the difference between the right word and a funky sounding mistake.

It is unclear as to how the dieresis came about in Spanish. Nevertheless, it is utilized in other languages. So, if you happen to be familiar with these accents in other languages, then you shouldn't be entirely surprised by their inclusion in Spanish.

The third type of accent is the "vergulilla." This is the accent above the "ñ." This is the only accent used on a consonant in Spanish. No other consonant has an accent placed on it. As noted earlier, the /en-yeh/ sound clear differentiates it from the /n/ sound. Just like the dieresis, it is unclear as to how the "ñ" emerged in Spanish. It is widely accepted as a part of countless numbers of accents that were initially used in Spanish writing. Over time, Spanish writing was simplified, leaving the "ñ" on the books for practical reasons.

Uses of the Tilde

As you dig deeper into your Spanish studies, you will find that there are some rather complex orthographic rules that go into the use of Spanish. With the intent of simplifying things, we have compiled a list of cases where the use of the tilde is certain.

- Words that end in "ción" and "sión" will always carry a tilde on the "o." Examples are "conclusión" and "confirmación." Leaving the tilde off is considered to be a spelling mistake in this case.
- Verbs in the past tense, such as "jugué" (I played) and "dormí" (I slept) are good examples. Virtually, all verbs in the past tense will end in a tilde on the final consonant. This is a phonological device used to highlight clearly the tense of the verb.
- Verbs with the "ía" ending are another example. These verbs are roughly equivalent to the "would + verb" combination in English. For instance, "jugaría" (would play) and "dormía" (would sleep) are solid examples.
- Next, a verb in the future simple will also have a tilde on the final syllable. For example, "jugaré" (I will play) and "dormiré" (I will sleep) highlight this type of verb conjugation. Nevertheless, keep in mind that while "jugué" and "dormiré" both end in the same "é" vowel, they are completely different tenses.
- Then, there are "long" words that carry tildes in the middle of the word. These "long" words carry a tilde since they have more than four syllables. As such, the tilde is needed in order to guide the reader as to the proper pronunciation of the word. For instance, "demostrándole" (showing him) or "insertándolos" (inserting them) are words which could potentially be confusing if they didn't have the accent attached to them.
- Most words that carry the stress on the final syllable have a tilde on that syllable. This is intended to avoid any potential confusion in the word's pronunciation. Some examples include, "bebé" (baby), japonés (Japanese), "maíz) (maize, corn). On that note, nationalities that end in "nés" will always carry a tilde. By the way, nationalities are not capitalized in Spanish. Of course, not every single word that carries the stress in the final syllable has a tilde, but this is a good, general rule of thumb.
- Be on the lookout for names and surnames that carry a tilde. In legal terms, it is not required for names to carry tilde unless they are legally spelled that way. For instance, "Fernández" and "Fernandez" would be pronounced the same, though legally, it may be spelled without the tilde. This could be due to a clerical error. So, keep in mind that if an accentuated name or surname is spelled without the mark, it could be due to a legal issue.

The official ruling body on the use of tildes is the RAE. What this means is that if you are ever in doubt with the use of a tilde, there is the place where you can go. In general, the RAE dictionary is the official sources whenever you have any doubt on the spelling of a word of the conjugation of a verb. So, it certainly pays to keep this in mind.

Perhaps the best way to improve your use of accents is through reading. The more you read, the more you will notice which words carry an accent and which ones do not. This will allow you to become more familiar with the way that Spanish accents work.

At the end of the day, proper spelling and accentuation can be learned through constant practice. The guidelines in this chapter are meant to make the entire process as simple as possible. So now it's just a matter of practicing these points so that you can make the most of your practice time.

Chapter 8: The Use of Numbers, Colors, Time and Feelings

Counting in Spanish

Let's begin this chapter with the use of numbers. The number system in Spanish is based on a ten base (other languages, such as French, use numbers on a sixty base). This makes the numerical structure of Spanish rather similar to English. The first twenty digits are unique. After twenty, numbers all follow the same pattern until reaching one-hundred. After one-hundred, the same pattern repeats over and over until reaching one-thousand.

Let's have a look at the first ten numbers, including zero.

Spanish	English
0 = cero	Zero
1 = uno	One
2 = dos	Two
3 = tres	Three
4 = cuatro	Four
5 = cinco	Five
6 = seis	Six
7 = siete	Seven
8 = ocho	Eight
9 = nueve	Nine
10 = diez	Ten

Table 2. Numbers from 0 to 10 in Spanish

The first ten digits, plus zero, don't bear much resemblance to each other, though they are structured in the same manner. So, it is a matter of learning each digit accordingly. Arabic numbers are also used. Consequently, there is no problem in expressing numbers in the same manner.

Numbers eleven to twenty in Spanish words are presented in Table 3.

Spanish	English
11 = once	Eleven
12 = twelve	Doce
13 = trece	Thirteen
14 = catorce	Fourteen
15 = quince	Fifteen
16 = dieciseis	Sixteen
17 = diecisiete	Seventeen
18 = dieciocho	Eighteen
19 = diecinueve	Nineteen
20 = veinte	twenty

Table 3. Numbers from 11 to 20 in Spanish

In this list, you can see how each number is spelled out to reflect its combination of digits. In the case of dieciseis, deicisiete, dieciocho, and diecinueve, you may find that these are spelled as "diez y seis" (ten and six), "diez y siete" (ten and seven), "diez y ocho" (ten and eight), and "diez y nueve" (ten and nine). These are accepted spellings, though they are not usually taught that way. The reason for this is based on a simplified system where remembering the correct spelling of these numbers is a lot easier that way. Nevertheless, you can spell these numbers both ways, which should not make a difference.

One important pronunciation note is that "quince" (15) is pronounced as /keen-seh/ and not /kwIns/. So please keep this in mind whenever you are referring to this number.

Next, the numbers for twenty to thirty still have their own particular spelling. Let's have a look.

Spanish	English
21 = veintiuno	Twenty-one
22 = veintidós	Twenty-two
23 = veintitrés	Twenty-three
24 = veinticuatro	Twenty-four
25 = venticinco	Twenty-five
26 = veintiseis	Twenty-six
27 = veintisiete	Twenty-seven
28 = veintiocho	Twenty-eight
29 = veintinueve	Twenty-nine
30 = treinta	thirty

Table 4. Numbers from 21 to 30 in Spanish

With this lot of numbers, you will find that they have a specific spelling. Nevertheless, it is accepted to spell them as "veinte y uno," "veinte y dos," and so on. Ultimately, it is up to you to find the form that is much easier for you. Also, note that "veintidós" and "veintitrés" carry a tilde for you to recognize the stress on the word's last syllable.

The remaining numbers from 30 onward can be spelled as "treinta y uno" and so on. This makes it rather easy to spell out the remaining numbers up to one-hundred. Here is a list of the remaining numbers in order of tens.

Spanish	English
40 = cuarenta	Forty
50 = cincuenta	Fifty
60 = sesenta	Sixty
70 = setenta	Seventy
80 = ochenta	Eighty
90 = noventa	Ninety
100 = cien	One hundred
200 = doscientos	Two hundred
300 = trescientos	Three hundred
1000 = mil	One thousand

Table 5. Numbers from 40 to 1000 in Spanish

In this chart, you will notice how each ten is based on a single digit. So, "cuatro" becomes "cuarenta" and so on. Also, one hundred is spelled out as "cien." However, when combined with the remaining digits, the numbers would work out a "ciento uno" (101), "ciento dos" (102), and so on. What this means is that you can combine "ciento" with any other number. As such, "ciento treinta y nueve" (139) can be spelled out just like the earlier ones.

Also, "mil" is one thousand and can be combined as follows:

- Diez mil (ten thousand)
- Cien mil (one-hundred thousand)
- Un millón (one million)
- Diez millones (ten million)
- Mil millones (one billion)

Notice how "billion" is expressed as a "thousand million," though it is possible to say "un billon." Both forms would be understood, though "thousand million" would be more suitable for a formal business context.

Describing With Colors

Next, we have colors. One very important note about numbers is that, like all adjectives, colors are subject to the masculine-feminine agreement, as well as singular and plural agreement. This means that you need to make sure that the color agrees with the subject you are talking about.

First, let's have a list of the most commonly used colors.

Spanish	English
Amarillo	Yellow
Anaranjado	Orange
Azul	Blue
Blanco	White
Gris	Grey
Marron	Brown
Morado	Purple
Negro	Black
Rojo	Red
Rosado	Pink
Verde	Green

Table 6. Most commonly used colors in Spanish

By default, colors are masculine. But when they agree with a feminine subject, their spelling changes. For example, "vestido rosado" (pink dress) refers to a masculine noun (vestido). So, "rosado" is spelled with an "o" ending. In the case of a feminine noun, "camisa rosada" (pink shirt), "camisa" is considered feminine. As such, "rosada" now has an "a" ending in order to signal that it is feminine and not masculine.

The situation changes somewhat when you factor in singular and plural. So, "vestidos rosados" (pink dresses) agrees both in terms of gender and number. The "s" ending indicates that it is plural. In the case of "camisas rosadas," the same situation applies.

Notice also that both the adjective and noun must be singular or plural in order to maintain the proper agreement.

There are a couple of exceptions, though. Azul, gris, verde, and marrón do not change in terms of gender but do agree in terms of number. So, "botas grises" (grey boots), where "botas" is feminine plural, would be the same as "coches grises" (grey cars), where "coches" is masculine plural.

Please keep this in mind, as there are exceptions from time to time. Bear in mind that virtually all adjectives in Spanish have a singular and plural form, even if they are considered uncountable in English. For instance, "un pan" (a bread) may refer to individual units of bread in Spanish, where "bread" in uncountable in English.

Also, in Spanish, adjectives come after nouns. So, "cielo azul" (blue sky) is the opposite of the proper English syntax. Please keep this in mind so that you can avoid confusing your interlocutors when speaking.

Telling the Time

The next topic covered in this chapter is time.

Time is a rather straightforward topic in Spanish. However, there are a couple of differences.

For starters, time is generally based on a 24-hour clock rather than two, 12-hour clocks. So, the morning hours are expressed from "cero horas" (zero hours, or midnight) to "doce horas" (twelve hours, or midday). After midday, time is expressed as "trece horas" (thirteen hours), all the way up to "veinticuatro horas" or midnight. Once the new day begins, time is then reset to "zero hours." This distinction is made in order to avoid confusion between am and pm times.

For instance, if you have an appointment at 7 o'clock in the evening, you could express it at "diecinueve horas en punto" (nineteen hours "on point"). The expression, "on point" is used to indicate that it is the beginning of the hour or "o'clock" in English.

It is also possible to express time on a 12-hour basis. However, it is important to include the specific time of day you are referring to. So, "ten o'clock in the morning" would be "diez de la mañana." Afternoon hours would be referred to as "de la tarde." For instance, "cinco de la tarde" (17:00 or 5 pm) is referring to a time that is past midday.

Now, here is an interesting difference between English and Spanish. Spanish does not account for "evening." As a matter of fact, as soon as the sun goes down and it gets dark, the time then becomes "noche" or night. So, "seis de la tarde" would be "six in the afternoon" since the sun doesn't typically finish setting by this time. However, "siete de la noche" (seven at night) would be logical since it is normal for it to be dark around this time. So, the rule of thumb is that as soon as it is completely dark, you can begin to use "night."

This also applies to greetings, like "goodnight" or "buenas noches," which is the applicable greeting whenever it is completely dark. However, if there is still a twinge of sunlight, then it would still be proper to use "buenas tardes" (good afternoon).

Fractional portions of hours also have their own particular expressions.

- "cuarto" refers to "quarter." So, "es un cuarto después de las dos" (it's a quarter past two) refers to 2:15. "Un cuarto para las dos," (a quater to two) refers to 1:45. Please notice the difference in the use of "después" (after) and "para" (to) when referring to time.
- Also, the use of "media" (half) makes it clear that you are talking about half hours. So, "son las tres y media" (It is three and a half) is the same as saying "half past," or 30 minutes past the hour.
- Other fractional hours can be expressed using the exact number of minutes. So, "es la una y venticinco" (it's one twenty-five) refers to 1:25.

- Please notice that hours are always expressed in the plural form, except for one. Hours are feminine, but minutes are masculine. Nevertheless, your expression of time will always make reference to the feminine form and not the masculine form.

When in doubt, you can always refer to time by expressing the numbers themselves. For example, you can say, "son las cuatro y cinco" (it's four and five), that is, 4:05. You will not be questioned if you are referring to am or pm when giving the current time, but you might be asked to clarify if you are referring to a future time. So, be sure to use "de la mañana," "de la tarde," or "de la noche" in order to clarify the time of day you are referring to.

Now, let us move on to the days of the week.

- lunes (Monday)
- martes (Tuesday)
- miércoles (Wednesday)
- jueves (Thursday)
- viernes (Friday)
- sábado (Saturday)
- domingo (Sunday)

Please note that the days of the week are not capitalized in Spanish. In fact, they are written in lowercase letters. For example, "hoy es lunes" (Today is Monday) illustrates how the days of the week are not capitalized.

Also, here are the months of the year.

- enero (January)
- febrero (February)
- marzo (March)
- abril (April)
- mayo (May)
- junio (June)
- july (Julio)
- agosto (August)
- septiembre (September)
- octubre (October)
- noviembre (November)
- diciembre (December)

Just like the days of the week, months are not written with capitals. So, a formal date such as "lunes, tres de septiembre" (Monday, September third) would not be expressed in capitals. Also, please note that dates are written out in nominal number and not in ordinal numbers like in the case of English.

With regard to years, there is no split between the digits of a year. For example, the year "2010" would be "dos mil diez," that is, "two thousand ten." So, keep this in mind any time you are talking about a year.

Here are some examples:

- 1991 (mil novecientos noventa y uno – one thousand nine hundred and ninety-one)
- 2002 (dos mil dos – two thousand two)
- 1885 (mil ochocientos ochenta y cinco – one thousand eight hundred and eighty-five)

Keep this important difference in mind when talking about years.

Expressing Feelings

The last item in this chapter refers to feelings.

Generally speaking, feelings are adjectives, which agree in gender and number. This implies that you need to be aware if you are talking about yourself or others in the singular and/or plural form.

As such, a question such as "¿Cómo estás?" (how are you?) can be replied with:

- Estoy bien. (I am fine)
- Estoy cansado/a (I am tired)
- Estoy feliz (I am happy)

Notice how "feliz" does not have a gender agreement but would have a plural agreement as "feliz" (singular) and "felices" (happy in plural form).

Here is a list of the most common feelings in the Spanish language.

Spanish	English
Feliz	Happy
Enamorado/a	In love
Aburrido/a	Bored
Cansado/a	Tired
Asustado/a	Scared
Enojado/a	Angry
Celoso/a	Jealous
Sorprendido/a	Surprised
Content/a	Happy, satisfied
Nervioso/a	Nervous
Ocupado/a	Busy
Preocupado/a	Worried
Furioso/a	Furious
Triste	Sad
Avergonzado/a	Embarrassed
Optimista	Optimistic
Relajado/a	Relaxed
Fatal	Terrible, awful

Table 7. Most commonly used colors in Spanish

Notice how most of the adjectives are presented as "o/a" in order to indicate their masculine or feminine form. There are a couple of exceptions, such as "feliz," "triste," and "optimista," which do not have a specific gender form. So, please make sure to use them without changing their ending. Nevertheless, they do have a singular and plural form. So, make sure to keep this in mind.

In the next chapter, we will dig deeper into the use of adjectives, nouns, and articles and how you can use the vocabulary covered in this chapter in order to make sentences and express your ideas in a clear manner.

Chapter 9: Nouns, Articles, and Adjectives

Adjectives

In the previous chapter, we discussed colors and feelings. This was our introduction to adjectives. As such, adjectives work the same way in Spanish as they do in English. Adjectives are used to describe nouns and even other adjectives.

Any number of words can qualify as adjectives: numbers, feelings, colors, materials, size, and other general descriptors. One very important difference between English and Spanish is that adjectives don't necessarily have a specific order which they must follow. This means is that you can basically list adjectives in any way that you feel makes sense and is understandable to your interlocutors.

So, let's take a look at how each type of adjective can be used in a conversation:

- **Numbers**. Numbers used to indicate quantity can be used like any other type of adjective. For instance, "un dólar" (one dollar) or "veinte dólares" (twenty dollars) can be used in this manner. Notice that "uno dólar" is not used but "un" is. This is done only when the number "uno" is used as an adjective to indicate quantity. Numbers do not agree in gender or have singular/plural forms.
- **Feelings**. As indicated in the previous chapter, feelings must agree in terms of number and gender. Also, mind the exceptions.
- **Colors**. As indicated in the previous chapter, colors must agree in terms of number and gender. Also, mind the exceptions.
- **Materials**. Materials, that is, what objects are made of, are also common adjectives. For instance, "lana" (wool) "madera" (wood), "cuero" (leather), "vidrio" (glass), "plástico" (plastic), and "metal" (metal) are the most common materials you can find. These materials are not gender-specific and don't have singular/plural agreement. So, "sillas de madera" (wooden chairs) has its plural noun (sillas), but the adjective (madera) remains singular. The reason for this is that you are using the preposition "de" to indicate the material that it is made of. As such, you are literally saying "chairs of wood."
- **Size**. Words, such as "pequeño" (small), "mediano" (medium), and "grande" (large) are common adjectives used to refer to size. In this case, you need to agree in terms of gender and number. So, "sillas pequeñas" (small chairs) agrees both in terms of gender and number. In the case of "grande," it is gender-neutral but must agree in terms of number. Other size-related adjectives include "chiquito" (tiny), "enorme" (enormous), "largo" (long), "corto" (short), "ancho" (wide), and "angosto" (narrow), which you can use.
- **General descriptors**. In this group, we can find phrases such as "Bueno" (good), "malo" (bad), and expressions, such as "excelente" (excellent) and "terrible" (terrible, awful) to use to describe people, things, and situations in general terms.

Here is a list of adjectives referring to personal qualities and characteristics, which you will surely find useful when describing people.

- Alto/a = tall

- Bajo/a = short
- Flaco/a = skinny
- Delgado/a = thin
- Gordo/a = fat
- Rubio/a = blonde
- Moreno/a = dark
- Pelirrojo/a = redhead

Once again, you will notice that there is the need to ensure agreement in both terms of gender and number.

Articles

The next item to be covered in this chapter deals with articles. In Spanish, articles are related to both gender and number.

So, let's look at the articles related to gender.

In the singular form, the masculine singular article is "el." Please note that the pronoun "él" refers to "he." In this case, the difference is the tilde on the "e." This serves no other purpose but to differentiate the article from the pronoun.

In the case of the feminine singular, the pronoun used is "la." For example, "la luna" (the moon) makes it clear that you are talking about the singular form of a feminine noun. By the same token, "el sol" (the sun) is masculine. As such, it is masculine and singular, hence the use of "el."

So, anytime you are referring to singular nouns, it is important to keep in mind that they will use either "el" or "la," depending on their gender. There are no gender-neutral nouns in Spanish. That is why it is important to keep in mind that even objects will have a gender assigned to them.

The general rule of thumb is to look out for the ending in their names. As such, nouns that end in "o" are typically masculine, while nouns ending in "a" are generally feminine. Of course, there are several exceptions. For example, "el agua" (water) is actually masculine, while "la radio" (radio) are exceptions to the rule.

The best piece of advice, in this case, is to make sure that you take note of the gender assigned to the various words you run into. That way, you can become familiar with both the general rules and the exceptions.

The plural articles play off the singular ones. So, "el" (masculine singular) will be "los" (masculine plural). For instance, "el coche" (the car) is a singular, masculine noun. "Los coches" (the cars) would be its plural form. In this manner, singular, masculine nouns will take the plural form they need.

With regard to feminine nouns, "la computadora" (the computer) will then become "las computadoras" in the plural, feminine form. Just like the masculine form, the article changes, along with the addition of the letter "s" at the end of it. This makes the agreement work perfectly as per Spanish orthographic rules.

To sum up, these are masculine and feminine articles:

- "el" (the, masculine, singular)
- "los" (the, masculine, singular)
- "la" (the, feminine, singular)
- "las" (the, feminine, singular)

Also, note that the indefinite article "a/an" in English is not used in Spanish. If you are referring to a singular object, you can use "un" (one) to refer to it.

Nouns

The third item in this chapter pertains to nouns.

In Spanish, nouns work in exactly the same way as they do in English. Nouns are a person, place, or thing. As such, there is not much guesswork in this regard.

On the whole, nouns can be classified as common nouns, proper nouns, abstract, concrete, individual, and collective.

Common nouns are those which refer to any person, place, or thing that is not the official name of it. For instance, "perro" (dog), "aire" (aire), and "lápiz" (pencil) are some examples of common nouns.

Proper nouns are the official names of people, countries, and titles. Names such as Juan, Pedro, María, and Teresa are just some examples. If a name is not typically Spanish and imported into Spanish, they must still be capitalized. The same goes for surnames, regardless of their origin. Names of countries are capitalized, but nationalities are not. So, "Alemania" (Germany) is capitalized as it is the name of a country, but "alemán" (German) is not capitalized as it refers to the nationality. Street names are also capitalized.

Other nouns which are not capitalized in Spanish are days of the week and months of the year. So, "lunes" (Monday) is not capitalized just as "marzo" (March) is not.

Here is a quick list of the days of the week:

- lunes (Monday)
- martes (Tuesday)
- miércoles (Wednesday)
- jueves (Thursday)
- viernes (Friday)
- sábado (Saturday)
- domingo (Sunday)

Here are the months of the year.

- enero (January)
- febrero (February)
- marzo (March)
- abril (April)
- mayo (May)
- junio (June)
- julio (July)

- agosto (August)
- septiembre (September)
- octubre (October)
- noviembre (November)
- diciembre (December)

As far as concrete and abstract nouns go, these are nouns which can either be physically perceived in some way or not. For example, "gato" (cat) is a concrete noun as it can be perceived and physically exists while "justiciar" (justice) is an idea which is considered a noun but does not have an actual, physical manifestation.

Collective and individual nouns are another term for singular and plural nouns. However, there are nouns which are considered to be individual and others which are considered to be collective. For instance, "mujer" (woman) is an individual noun as it represents one, individual woman. On the other hand, "flota" (fleet) refers to a group of ships. As such, it is collective. Now, you might see "la flota" (the fleet) and think it is singular, which is true, but it is collective nonetheless, as it is referring to a group of ships.

If you are ever in doubt about whether a noun is singular, plural, collective, and so on, the RAE online dictionary can help you determine the official form of a word. The RAE is the definitive party on this matter. So, feel free to consult it any time you are unsure or unclear about any terms in Spanish.

Chapter 10: Plurals

In Spanish, both nouns and adjectives are plurals. So, you need to make sure that both adjectives and nouns agree when you are constructing a sentence. While we have gone over some of the most important aspects of the plural form in previous chapters, we are now going to focus on the guidelines that come with building plurals in Spanish.

Word Ending in a Vowel

Nouns and adjectives that end in a vowel should have an "s" added to them. This is applicable to any noun or adjective that ends in a vowel, "a," "e," "i," "o," or "u." Some examples include:

- Silla (chair) – sillas (chairs)
- Teléfono (telephone) – teléfonos (telephones)
- Taxi (cab) – taxis (cabs)
- Buque (boat) – buques (boats)
- Tribu (tribe) – tribus (tribes)

The same goes for words that end in an accentuated vowel, that is, with a tilde at the end of it. For example:

- Bebé (baby) – Bebés (babies)
- Papá (father) – papás (fathers/parents)
- Buró (office) – burós (offices)

However, in the case of "ú" and "í," "es" is added to make the plural form. For instance:

- Tabú (taboo) – tabúes (taboos)
- Colibrí (hummingbird) – colibríes (hummingbirds)

In this case, it is more of a pronunciation device than an orthographic one. As such, please pay attention to the words ending in "í" and "ú." The good news is that words with these endings are quite as common as the first group.

Also, the "í" ending is applicable to some demonyms. For example:

- paquistaní (Pakistaní) – paquistaníes (Pakistanis)
- iraní (Iranian) – iraníes (Iranians)
- iraquí (Iraqi) – iraquíes (Iraqis)

While most demonyms generally end in "iego" or "és," the "í" tends to be a bit of a special case. For other demonyms, you will add the "es" ending:

- danés (Dane) – danéses (Danes)
- finlandés (Finn) – finlandéses (finns)
- irlandés (Irish) – irlandéses (Irish)

Also,

- griego (Greek) – griegos (Greeks)

All other demonyms would just have the "s" added to it.

Words Ending in Consonants

In the case of words that end in "y," the "es" ending is required to make the plural form. For instance:

- ley (law) – leyes (laws)
- rey (king) – reyes (kings)
- lady (Lady, as in noble rank) – ladys (Ladies)

While the "y" ending isn't all that common, you will certainly run into a few words containing this ending.

Also, please bear in mind that all words ending in "s" (in singular form) and "x" shall have the "es" ending added to it.

For example:

- fax (fax) – faxes (faxes)
- compás (compass) – compáses (compasses)

Given the nature of the "s" being the plural ending, there aren't many words that end in "s" in their singular form. The ones that do don't generally change. For example:

- el virus – los virus
- el viernes – los Viernes
- la crisis – las crisis
- el tórax – los tórax

The previous examples illustrate how these words remain the same in their singular and plural forms. In addition, words ending in "z" will have the "es" ending added but with the "z" changing to "c." For instance:

- pez (fish) – peces (fish)
- voz (voice) – voces (voices)
- feroz (fierce) – feroces (fierce)

Words that end in "l," "r," n," "d," and "j," so long as they follow a vowel, will also have the "es" ending added to it.

Some examples of this rule are as follows:

- barril (barrel) – barriles (barrels)
- amor (loves) – amores (loves)
- camión (truck) – camiones (trucks)
- actividad (activity) – actividades (activities)
- reloj (clock) – relojes (clocks)

In addition, words ending in any other consonant that isn't the ones we have listed above would simply have "s" added to it. This is mainly due to pronunciation more than any orthographic reason. Here are some examples:

- álbum – álbums (albums)
- bóxer – bóxers (boxers, sport)
- cómic – cómics (comics)
- póster – pósters (posters)
- superávit – superávits (surpluses)

These words do not take the "es" ending in the plural form. It should be noted that these words are not nearly as common as those that take the "es" ending. Another thing to keep in mind is that the majority of these terms have been originally imported from other languages. As such, they tend to maintain the same structure from their original languages.

Nouns With Two or More Words and Proper Nouns

In the event of nouns that are made up of two or more words, all of the words need to become plural. This maintains the overall singular/plural structure of that noun. Consider the following examples:

- Los Estados Unidos (The United States)
- Las Naciones Unidas (The United Nations)
- Estados miembros (member states)
- Sus Majestades (Their Majesties)
- Sus Altezas Reales (Their Royal Highness)
- Buenos Aires (the city of Buenos Aires)

The above examples are generally limited to formal titles or designations. Nevertheless, each word that makes up the whole noun is plural, as it is part of the whole name, title, or designation.

Also, when you are talking about a family, the surname is not pluralized. So, if you are to the Smith family, you would have "los Smith." By the same token, the Rodríguez family would be "los Rodríguez." As such, surnames are never pluralized.

This previous point also applies to brand names. This is true in the event that you are referring to various objects by the brand and not their actual name, for example, los coches Toyota (the Toyota cars). In this example, you wouldn't pluralize the brand name, as it is a proper noun just like names and surnames. Consequently, you can pluralize the noun itself (car, in this case) but without pluralizing the brand. Here are some more examples:

- Zapatillas Nike (Nike sneakers)
- Chocolates Snickers (Snickers chocolates)
- Computadoras Dell (Dell computers)
- Relojes Omega (Omega watches)
- Gafas de sol Ray-Ban (Ray-Ban sunglasses)

Even if you referred to the items as if their brand was a noun, it would still not be pluralized. Take the example, "los Ford son muy buenos" (Fords are very good). While you would pluralize the brand name in English, you wouldn't do so in Spanish, especially if their brand name is originally from another language.

The same concept extends to the name of companies. When a company opens several branches or offices, such as in the case of banks, you won't use the company's name in the plural form. You would only limit yourself to expressing the name of the company in relation to the number of offices opened. For example, "han abierto tres nuevos Walmart en la ciudad" (Three new Walmarts have been opened). The main reasoning behind this rule is that it is hard to determine what the proper plural form would be. So, it is much easier to keep the name as singular. In the event that you do hear people refer to companies and brands in the plural form, it might be due to colloquialisms from locals more than actual grammatical logic.

Chapter 11: Pronouns

In Spanish, pronouns have the same function as they do in English. The main function of a pronoun is to substitute a common or proper noun. In that regard, pronouns are used to take the place of nouns in the subject or object position.

Personal Pronouns

So, let's first dive into the pronouns in the subject position. This is where personal pronouns come into play. In Spanish, subject pronouns function in the same way as they do in English but do have a bit of a different structure.

- Yo (I)
- Tú (you informal, singular)
- Usted (you formal, singular)
- Él (he, singular)
- Ella (she, singular)
- Nosotros (we, plural)
- Ellos (they masculine, plural)
- Ellas (they feminine, plural)
- Ustedes (you, plural)

As you can see, the structure of subject pronouns is essentially the same in Spanish as they are in English. However, there are some differences. These differences are related to the very essence and nature of the language.

For starters, you will notice that there are two forms of "you." The first form; that is, "tú" is the informal version. This can be used among friends, family, peers, colleagues, and anyone with whom you are on a friendly basis. In most countries, it is not recommended to use this form when addressing strangers. As such, "tú" is used when you have some type of relationship with a person that is not based on a hierarchical context. For example, it is uncommon to use "tú" with your boss or superiors unless you are invited to do so.

It is quite common for men of the same age and rank to use this form among themselves. However, men should take care of not automatically using this form to address women, especially if they are in a formal business context.

So, if you find yourself in a formal context, "usted" is the best way to go. This form can be used to address strangers in public places and with people who are older or have a higher rank than you. For instance, if you are addressing public officials, these individuals have a higher rank and therefore, command respect even if it is simply a social convention.

A good example of this is the military. Officers of higher rank would address those of lower rank by using "tú." However, those soldiers of lower rank would have to address their superiors by using "usted" as a sign of respect for the rank and office they hold.

Another interesting difference is the lack of a gender-neutral pronoun. As such, "it" does not exist in Spanish since every single noun is assigned a gender. Consequently, all objects, including animals, must be referred to with its corresponding gender.

There is also the use of "ellos" and "ellas" in reference to "they." Given the fact that English does not assign gender, only one pronoun is necessary. In this case, please bear in mind that there is a clear distinction when referring to the gender of nouns in the plural form.

Also, the use of "ustedes" as the plural form of "you" makes a clear distinction for the singular and plural forms of "you." This is a significant difference with English as English does not contemplate a plural version of "you."

As you gain experience with Spanish, you may encounter the use of "vos" and "vosotros." These two forms are not widely used in Latin America. In fact, their use is limited to a handful of countries. "Vos" is the third form of "you," which is considered to be very informal. It marks the lowest level formality when addressing other folks. It is widely used in Argentina and Uruguay while used in Colombia but only when forming close relationships with people of similar age and rank. In Central America, the use of "vos" is rather common, though it is only used when there is absolute confidence among people. It is seldomly used between men and women, though it is quite common among siblings.

"Vosotros" is the plural form of "vos." It is an informal way of referring to a group of people. However, it is basically used in Spain and considered archaic in Latin America. As such, you will hear this form used rather commonly in Spain but almost never in Latin America. In fact, if you were to use it in Latin America, you would get some funny looks from your interlocutors since it isn't all that common.

When referring to pronouns in the object position, that is, following the verb, the same batch of personal pronouns can be used in this context. For example, "Ella le habla a él" literally means "she speaks to he." In English, the proper form would be "She speaks to him." However, Spanish does not use a specific set of object pronouns in the same manner that English does. So, in a manner of speaking, it is a much simpler grammatical construct.

Possessive Pronouns

Next, we have possessive pronouns. These have the same function as they do in English. Let's take a look at these.

Personal	Possessive	English
Yo (I)	Mi	My
Tú (you informal, singular)	Tu	Your
Usted (you formal, singular)	Su	Your
Él (he, singular)	Su	His
Ella (she, singular)	Su	Her
Nosotros (we, plural)	Nuestro	Our
Ellos (they masculine, plural)	Su	Their
Ellas (they feminine, plural)	Su	Their
Ustedes (you, plural)	Su	Your

Table 8. Personal and possessive pronouns in Spanish

As you can see, the use of "su" can be used when referring to "usted," "él," and "ella," while "su" is also used as the plural form of these pronouns. Now, there are a couple of interesting differences.

Firstly, "tu," without a tilde, is the possessive pronoun form, whereas, "tú" with the tilde is "you." So, please be aware of this difference. While there is no difference in the pronunciation of either word, there is an orthographic function in this spelling difference.

Another key difference is that possessive pronouns are also subject to singular-plural agreement. So, if the object that agrees with the possessive pronoun (not the subject of the sentence) is plural, then the pronoun must also be plural. For instance, "Aquí están mis botas" (my boots are here), "mi" would be transformed into "mis." The same goes for "tu," as it becomes "tus" and "su" then changes to "tus." Also, "nuestro" becomes "nuestros." At the end of the day, all you need to do is add an "s" to make it plural.

Demonstrative Pronouns

Another batch of pronouns is known as "demonstrative pronouns." Here they are:

- Éste (this) – masculine
- Ésta (this) – feminine
- Éstos (these) – plural
- Ésa (that) – feminine
- Ése (that) – masculine

- Ésos (those) – plural
- Aquél (that) – masculine
- Aquélla (that) – feminine
- Aquéllos (those) – masculine plural
- Aquéllas (those) – feminine plural

Notice how these pronouns are equivalent to "this," "that," "these," and "those," though they do make a difference in terms of gender and number. Now, the basic difference between "ése" and "aquél" is the relative distance between the object and the speaker. For example, an object that is just beyond the speaker's reach would be "ése," while an object that is much farther away would be deemed as "aquél."

Also, please note that "ése," "ésa," "éste," and "ésta" are considered inappropriate for people. As such, they can be considered to be rude. So, when referring to a person, it is better to use "aquél" or "aquélla." Nevertheless, out of politeness, it is best to use a person's name or title rather than a pronoun.

You might hear "ése," for instance, used to refer to people. However, this pronoun is used either in a very informal context or even in a derogatory tone. So, please be on the lookout for such usage.

On the whole, you will find that the use of pronouns in Spanish is very similar to English. While there are some differences in terms of gender and number, the underlying concept is the same. So, do take the time to go over them and become familiar with their use in conversation.

Chapter 12: Verbs

Regular Verbs

In this chapter, we are going to focus on the use of verbs in the present simple tense. As such, we are going to be looking at verb conjugations and the patterns that come with the various types of verbs.

First, the key to conjugation Spanish verbs is based on the end of the verb in its infinitive form. It should be noted that the infinitive form means that the verb does not have a tense, i.e., past, present, or future.

There are three endings to all Spanish verbs in their infinitive form: AR, ER, and IR.

As such, all Spanish verbs will have one of these endings. Here are some examples:

- ER ending
    - Comer (to eat)
    - Conocer (to know)
    - Entender (to understand)
    - Volver (to return)
    - Responder (to respond)
- IR ending
    - Vivir (to live)
    - Sentir (to feel)
    - Permitir (to permit)
    - Confundir (to confuse)
    - Exigir (to demand)
- AR ending
    - Cargar (to load)
    - Hablar (to speak)
    - Arreglar (to arrange)
    - Jugar (to play)
    - Andar (to go)

The conjugation for these verbs follows a similar pattern, though there is a slight variation based on the ending. These variations are due more to pronunciation issues rather than grammatical concerns. Nevertheless, you will see that they are very similar and should soon become second nature to you as you gain more practice and experience.

Let us see the conjugation patterns for the ER-ending verbs below.

- Verb: Comer (to eat)
    - Yo com**o** (I eat)
    - Tú com**es** (you eat)
    - Usted com**e** (you eat)
    - Él com**e** (he eats)
    - Ella com**e** (they eat)
    - Nosotros com**emos** (we eat)

- Ellos com**en** (they eat)
- Ellas com**en** (they eat)
- Usteded com**en** (you eat)

As you can see, the ER ending is dropped in favor of the proper ending based on the subject pronoun in question. In the case of "yo," an "o" is added. So, that basically means that you only drop the "r" from the ending of the verb and switch the "e" for an "o." In the case of "tú," an "es" is added. As for you "usted," "él," and "ella," an "e" is added to the ending. "Nosotros" requires the addition of "emos," while "ellos," "ellas," and "ustedes" get the "en" ending.

That's basically it. The rest of the verbs will have some variations to them. Nevertheless, the basic pattern is the same.

Let's have a look at the verbs ending in IR:

- Verb: vivir (to live)
    - Yo viv**o** (I live)
    - Tú viv**es** (you live)
    - Usted viv**e** (you live)
    - Él viv**e** (he lives)
    - Ella viv**e** (he lives)
    - Nosotros viv**imos** (we live)
    - Ellos viv**en** (they live)
    - Ellas viv**en** (they live)
    - Ustedes viv**en** (you live)

As you can see, the pattern is the same as the exception in the conjugation of "nosotros." In this case, the "emos" ending is modified slightly to "imos." Aside from that, the rest of the endings are exactly the same.

Now, let's take a look at the AR endings:

- Verb: hablar (to speak)
    - Yo habl**o** (I speak)
    - Tú habl**as** (you speak)
    - Usted habl**a** (you speak)
    - Él habl**a** (he speaks)
    - Ella habl**a** (she speaks)
    - Nosotros habl**amos** (we speak)
    - Ellos habl**an** (they speak)
    - Ellas habl**an** (they speak)
    - Ustedes habl**an** (you speak)

With this verb ending, there are slight differences. First, with the "tú" conjugation, the verb changes from "es" to "as." Also, in the "nosotros" conjugation, the verb ending changes from "emos" or "imos" to "amos." Also, the "en" endings are changed to "an." These changes are due to the fact that the verb ends in AR. Hence, the endings reflect the change in pronunciation, as opposed to a specific grammar rule. Nevertheless, the pattern

remains the same. As such, you can easily get into the mechanics of conjugating these verbs.

Irregular Verbs

The conjugation patterns mentioned above are related to regular verbs. That means that there is a list of irregular verbs which you need to become familiar with. While this list is rather small, it contains some of the most common verbs you will use in conversation.

Let's take a look at the list:

- Dar (to give)
- Decir (to say)
- Estar (to be)
- Hacer (to do)
- Ir (to go)
- Oir (to hear)
- Pedir (to ask)
- Poder (can)
- Poner (to put)
- Querer (to want)
- Saber (to know)
- Seguir (to follow)
- Ser (to be)
- Tener (to have)
- Venir (to come)
- Ver (to see)

As you can see, all of these verbs maintain the AR, ER, and IR structure in their infinitive form. However, their structure makes it rather difficult to follow the same pattern that regular verbs follow. So, let's take a look at how these verbs are conjugated.

Person	dar	decir	estar	hacer	ir	oir	pedir	poder
Yo	doy	digo	estoy	hago	voy	oigo	pido	puedo
Tú	das	dices	estás	haces	vas	oyes	pides	puedes
Usted	da	dice	está	hace	va	oye	pide	puede
Él	da	dice	está	hace	va	oye	pide	puede
Ella	da	dice	está	hace	va	oye	pide	puede
Nosotros	damos	decimos	estamos	hacemos	vamos	oímos	pedimos	podemos
Ellos	dan	dicen	están	hacen	van	oyen	piden	pueden
Ellas	dan	dicen	están	hacen	van	oyen	piden	pueden
Ustedes	dan	dicen	están	hacen	van	oyen	piden	pueden

Person	poner	querer	saber	seguir	ser	tener	venir	ver
Yo	pongo	quiero	sé	sigo	soy	tengo	vengo	veo
Tú	pones	quieres	sabes	segues	eres	tienes	vienes	ves
Usted	pone	quiere	sabe	sigue	es	tiene	viene	ve
Él	pone	quiere	sabe	sigue	es	tiene	viene	ve
Ella	pone	quiere	sabe	sigue	es	tiene	viene	ve
Nosotros	ponemos	queremos	sabemos	seguimos	somos	temenos	venimos	vemos
Ellos	ponen	quieren	saben	siguen	son	tienen	vienen	ven
Ellas	ponen	quieren	saben	siguen	son	tienen	vienen	ven
Ustedes	ponen	quieren	saben	siguen	son	tienen	vienen	ven

Table 9. Irregular verbs in Spanish conjugated in the present simple.

The list above is intended to serve as a reference. As such, you will be able to use this table when you are going through verb lists and exercises. Please note that the structure does not vary significantly with each verb. Nevertheless, they do vary enough, so you need to pay attention to the way each of the verbs is written out.

Another note is if you are unsure whether a verb is irregular, you can assume that it is regular. The chances of a verb being irregular are far less than being regular. That is why the best piece of advice you can take into consideration at this point is that practice makes perfect. As you gain more practice and experience with verbs, you will easily recognize the patterns among regular and irregular verbs, so the amount of trouble you will have while figuring your conjugations will be far less than you had imagined initially.

Chapter 13: Ser and Estar

"Ser" and "estar" are the two most important verbs in the Spanish language. They serve as both verbs and auxiliaries within the various tenses. That is why we have devoted an entire chapter to discussing both verbs.

First of all, both "ser" and "estar" translate into "to be" in English. What this means is that if you look them up, they will both be reflected as "to be." So, what's the difference?

There are two main differences between each one. The first is that "ser" refers to things that are considered permanent or that are unlikely to change. This applies to personal information, such as your name, address, nationality, and so on. While any of these bits of information could potentially change, it is highly unlikely that they will.

"Estar" refers to states, which by definition, are considered less permanent. Feelings are a prime example. Since your feelings are much more likely to change, "estar" would be the verb of choice. "Estar" does have one other important function; it is used as an auxiliary verb, especially when constructing continuous tenses. As such, you can use it in combination with the main verb of the sentence in order to produce the tense you wish to use.

Ser — "to be"

So, let's begin by looking at the conjugation of "ser."

- Yo soy (I am)
- Tú eres (you are)
- Usted es (you are)
- Él es (he is)
- Ella es (she is)
- Nosotros somos (we are)
- Ellos son (they are)
- Ellas son (they are)
- Ustedes son (you are)

With this in mind, you can express ideas such as the following:

- Yo soy de Alemania. (I am from Germany)
- Tú eres un turista. (You are a tourist)
- Usted es mi amiga. (You are my friend)
- Él es amigable. (He is friendly)
- Ella es interesante. (She is interesting)
- Nosotros somos nuevos estudiantes. (We are new students)
- Ellos son los mejores trabajadores. (They are the best workers)
- Ellas son mis hermanas. (They are my sisters)
- Ustedes son especiales. (You are special)

In all of these examples, we can see how we are either making a general description or stating a fact about this person. Granted, saying something like, "Él es amigable" isn't

exactly a fact but an opinion. Nevertheless, we are stating a personal characteristic or trait about this person. As such, we would use the "ser" version of "to be."

Also, note that in case where you are referring to a plural subject, adjectives and nouns must agree with that subject. Hence, "ellas son mis hermanas" means that "mis" and "hermanas" need to be in the plural form in order to make sense of the subject which you are utilizing.

Estar — "to be"

Now, in the case of "estar," things shift from discussing permanent states to more changeable ones. For instance, feelings, current arrangements, and other changing circumstances are expressed by using "estar."

So, let's have a look at the conjugation of this verb:

- Yo estoy (I am)
- Tú estás (you are)
- Usted está (you are)
- Él está (he is)
- Ella está (she is)
- Nosotros estamos (we are)
- Ellos están (they are)
- Ellas están (they are)
- Ustedes están (you are)

In this case, you can see that the English version of this verb is exactly the same, though there is a clear difference in the Spanish conjugation. As such, you need to keep an eye out when using "estar," as opposed to "ser."

Consequently, you can make sentences such as the following:

- Yo estoy cansada. (I am tired)
- Tú estás aquí. (You are here)
- Usted está confundido. (You are confused)
- Él está en casa. (He is at home)
- Ella está enferma. (She is sick)
- Nosotros estamos en camino. (We are on the way)
- Ellos están locos. (They are crazy)
- Ellas están seguras. (They are sure)
- Ustedes están en lo correcto. (You are right)

As you can see, the above examples with the "estar" verb refer to feelings, location, and other states. You can use this verb to indicate more about the subject of the sentence, be it a person or an object.

The other important use of "estar" lies with the present continuous. In Spanish, the present continuous has the same function as in English; that is, to talk about actions that are happening at the time of speaking or temporary actions that are taking place around the present time.

Consequently, "estar" is used as an auxiliary, while the main verb of the sentence is transformed from its infinitive form to the "ando" or "iendo" form. The good news is that there is only one conjugation for the main verb since the agreement with the subject takes place with the verb "estar" and not the main verb.

Consider this example:

- Nosotros estamos estudiando inglés. (We are studying English)

In this example, notice how "estudiar" (study) is transformed from its infinitive form to the present participle form "estudiando." When placed together with the "estar" form of the verb, the present continuous is formed.

It should be noted that the present continuous form is used to talk about future actions in English. This function is not used in Spanish. So, please keep in mind that the present continuous in Spanish is limited to the present only.

Now, take note of how the present participle is conjugated through these examples:

- In the case of AR-ending verbs, add "ando" to the verb's ending. For example:
    - Jugar (to play) – jugando (playing)
    - Ahorrar (to save) – ahorrando (saving)
    - Hablar (to speak) – hablando (speaking)
    - Amar (to love) – amando (loving)
    - Gustar (to like) – gustando (liking)
- In the case of IR-ending verbs, add "iendo" to the verb's ending. For example:
    - Vivir (to live) – viviendo (living)
    - Mentir (to lie) – mintiendo (lying)
    - Sentir (to feel) – sintiendo (feeling)
    - Abolir (to abolish) – aboliendo (abolishing)
    - Abrir (to open) – abriendo (opening)
- In the case of ER-ending verbs, add "iendo" to the verb's ending. For example:
    - Correr (to run) – corriendo (running)
    - Comer (to eat) – comiendo (eating)
    - Hacer (to do) – hacienda (doing)
    - Entender (to understand) – entendiendo (understanding)
    - Querer (to want) – queriendo (wanting)

At this point, let's take a look at some real-life examples:

- Yo estoy viajando a Europa. (I am traveling to Europe)
- Tú estás viendo televisión. (You are watching television)
- Usted está hablando por teléfono. (You are speaking on the telephone)
- Él está jugando basquetbol. (He is playing basketball)
- Ella está escuchando música. (She is listening to music)
- Nosotros estamos comiendo en un restaurante. (We are eating at a restaurant)
- Ellos están estudiando matemáticas. (They are studying mathematics)
- Ellas están durmiendo en el coche. (They are sleeping in the car)
- Ustedes están comprando ropa. (You are buying clothes)

These examples all illustrate how the present continuous can be structured in order to talk about actions that are happening right at the time of speaking. However, the present continuous can also be used to talk about temporary actions.

Consider these examples:

- Yo estoy trabajando en una oficina. (I am working at an office)
- Él está viviendo en un departamento. (he is living in an apartment)
- Nosotros estamos estudiando inglés. (we are studying English)

Each of the previous examples serves to indicate that the action being discussed is temporary. As such, if the action described was meant to indicate a more permanent condition, then the present simple would be used. For instance:

- Yo trabajo en una oficina. (I work at an office)
- Él vive en un departamento. (he lives in an apartment)
- Nosotros estudiamos inglés. (we study English)

Consequently, the use of the present simple makes it clear that this is a situation that is unlikely to change any time soon. Therefore, using both tenses makes a clear distinction as to what you are trying to convey to your interlocutor.

At this point, it is worth mentioning how important getting a firm grasp of the "ser" and "estar" verbs really is. By gaining a good understanding of their functioning, you will be able to construct useful sentences and even begin to play around with the language in such a way that you can transmit the information that you want to get across in an accurate manner. So, it certainly pays to take the time to master these two essential verbs.

Chapter 14: Question Formation

In the Spanish language, there are two main types of questions: open-ended questions and yes or no questions.

The expected answer is "yes" or "no" to a typical yes or no question, and this is probably a part of any language. Of course, the answer can be expanded beyond the simple "yes" or "no." Nevertheless, the end result is a short answer.

Yes-or-No Questions

In order to form a question of this nature, you can take a regular statement and flip the subject and verb from their regular positions. Consider this example:

- Él viaja a Europa cada verano. (He travels to Europe every summer)

This is a regular statement in the affirmative. Now, to change it into a yes/no question, we need to switch the subject and verb so that they can reflect the change in syntax. Here is the new word order used to reflect the question.

- ¿Viaja él a Europa cada verano? (Does he travel to Europe every summer??

First of all, notice how the subject "él" moves from the first spot to the second, and the verb from the second to the first. This change enables the formation of a yes/no question.

Now, the answer to this question can be constructed as follows:

- ¿Viaja él a Europa cada verano? (Does he travel to Europe every summer?)
    - Sí, él viaja. (Yes, he travels.)
    - No, él no viaja. (No, he doesn't travel.)

Please notice that the negative form is constructed by the use of "no." So, you can see that there is no other auxiliary used in Spanish to make the negative form. All you need is to use "no" in order to transform the sentence from positive to negative.

The answers presented above are short answers. Of course, you can elaborate on these responses as much as you like. Nevertheless, you could reply something like:

- Sí, él viaja a Europa cada verano. (Yes, he travels to Europe every summer.)
- No, él no viaja a Europa cada verano. (No, he doesn't travel to Europe every summer.)

These longer-form answers can be used to make a point or simply elaborate further on the question being asked. It is not a requisite for you to express your answers in this manner, though it is an option that you have at your disposal.

Below are more examples of questions in Spanish.

- Yo como frutas todos los días. – ¿Como yo frutas todos los días?
- *I eat fruit every day. – Do I eat fruit every day?*
- Tú juegas fútbol cada viernes. – ¿Juegas tú fútbol cada viernes?
- *You play soccer every Friday. – Do you play soccer every Friday?*

- Usted vende ropa en una tienda – ¿Vende usted ropa en una tienda?
- *You sell clothes in a shop. – Do you sell clothes in a shop?*
- Él vive en Chicago. – ¿Vive él en Chicago?
- *He lives in Chicago. – Does he live in Chicago?*
- Ella trabaja en una oficina – ¿Trabaja ella en una oficina?
- *She works in an office. – Does she work in an office?*
- Nosotros bebemos refrescos en la cena. – ¿Bebemos nosotros refrescos en la cena?
- *We drink soda at dinner. – Do we drink soda at dinner?*
- Ellos hacen ejercicio en el gimnasio. – ¿Hacen ellos ejercicio en el gimnasio?
- *They do exercise at the gym. – Do they exercise at the gym?*
- Ellas cocinan pasteles los fines de semana. – ¿Cocinan ellas pasteles los fines de semana?
- *They bake cakes on the weekend. – Do they bake cakes on the weekend?*
- Ustedes escuchan música en el coche. – ¿Escuchan ustedes música en el coche?
- *You listen to music in the car. – Do you listen to music in the car?*

One of the most interesting characteristics of Spanish is that you can omit the subject of the sentence only when it is clear what you are talking about or to whom you are referring. This comes in very handy when asking questions as it is very common for native Spanish speakers to drop the subject, especially when they are addressing you directly.

Let us have a look at the previous examples without the use of the subject in the sentence.

- ¿Trabajas en una oficina? (Do you work in an office?)
    - Sí, trabajo en una oficina. (Yes, I work in an office.)
    - No, no trabajo en una oficina. (No, I don't work in an office.)

As you can see in this example, it is not needed to say, "¿Trabajas tú en una oficina?" It is enough to say, "¿Trabajas en una oficina?" since it is clear that the question is being addressed to "you" and not to anyone else.

Now, it should be noted that when you omit the subject of a sentence or question, it is important to be clear about whom you are referring to. Otherwise, this could lead to confusion and cause your interlocutor to seek clarification. So, it pays to be extra careful in order to avoid any potential confusion.

Open-Ended Questions

From yes/no questions, we can move on to open-ended questions. These types of questions allow for any type of response and not just a limited yes/no reply. As such, we need to use the set of questions words available.

Here are the questions words used in Spanish:

- Qué (what)
- Quién (who)
- Cuál (which)
- Cuándo (when)
- Cuánto (how much/many)
- Cómo (how)

- Dónde (where)
- Por qué (why)

Please note that question words have a tilde attached to them in order to differentiate them from the relative pronouns. For instance, "cuando" is not the same as "cuándo." While their spelling and pronunciation are identical, the tilde differentiates their function in writing.

Consider this example:

- Compro pan y leche cuando voy al supermercado. (I buy bread and milk when I go to the supermarket.)

In this example, we are using "cuando" as a relative pronoun since it is joining two separate parts of a sentence. Also, we omitted the use of "yo" since the sentence makes absolutely clear that I am referring to myself and no one else.

The use of "cuándo" in a question would work out like this:

- ¿Cuándo compras pan? (When do you buy bread?)

In this case, we need to carry the tilde on "cuándo" so that it is absolutely clear that we are talking about a question. While the structure and the context don't really leave much room for doubt, it is, nevertheless, important to make the point to avoid potential confusion.

Let's look at some more sample questions:

- ¿Dónde es mi lugar? (Where is my place?)
- ¿Cuándo vas a la escuela? (When do you go to school?)
- ¿Cuántos años tiene? (How old are you?)
- ¿Quién es él? (Who is he?)
- ¿Qué bebe ella? (What does she drink?)
- ¿Por qué viajamos? (Why do we travel?)
- ¿Por qué trabajan ellos? (Why do they work?)
- ¿Cuál es la casa de ellas? (Which is their house?)
- ¿Cómo van al trabajo? (How do you get to work?)

There could be any number of responses to these questions. That is why they are open-ended. As such, it is up to you to find the right information that you would like to get across. For example:

- ¿Cuándo vas a la escuela? (When do you go to school?)
    - Voy a la escuela todos los días. (I go to school every day.)
    - Voy a la escuela en las noches. (I go to school at night.)
    - Voy a la escuela los fines de semana. (I go to school on weekends.)
    - No voy a la escuela. (I don't go to school.)

As you can see, the potential responses can vary according to the information you are looking to provide your interlocutors.

Let us examine some common questions that you will come across when speaking Spanish.

- ¿Cuál es tu nombre? (What is your name?)
- ¿De dónde eres? (Where are you from?)
- ¿Dónde vives? (Where do you live?)
- ¿Cuántos años tienes? (How old are you?)
- ¿Cuál es tu número de teléfono? (What is your telephone number?)
- ¿Dónde trabajas? (Where do you work?)
- ¿Cuál es tu correo electrónico? (What is your email?)
- ¿Cuál es tu trabajo? (What do you do?)
- ¿Dónde queda el banco? (Where is the bank?)
- ¿Dónde está el baño? (Where is the bathroom?)

These are the most common questions that you will encounter when you are speaking to other folks. As such, these questions can come through for you in a pinch. So, do take the time to go over them, and put them into practice as often as you need to.

On the whole, question formation is a matter of practice. The more practice you are able to get structuring questions, the better you will become at asking the right questions when you need to. Best of all, Spanish syntax is flexible enough to where you could mix up the word order and still get the message across.

Consequently, you can make the most of your opportunity to travel without having to hesitate about getting directions or interacting with other folks. As you gain more proficiency, you will be able to construct your own scenarios based on your specific needs. That is why this guide will come in handy when you need a reference point.

Chapter 15: Adverbs, Prepositions, and Conjunctions

Adverbs

Adverbs have the same essential function in Spanish as they do in English. Basically, adverbs are used to describe verbs, adjectives, and other adverbs. This is what makes them a rather versatile part of speech. In short, the use of adverbs in Spanish is all about providing additional information that gives the sentence greater clarity.

First, we are going to take a closer look at the adverbs of time. These adverbs clarify information regarding time, when something takes place and the frequency with which it takes place. Consider the following adverbs:

- A menudo (often)
- Ahora (now)
- Algunas veces (sometimes)
- Anteriormente (previously)
- Antes (before)
- Ayer (yesterday)
- Después (after)
- Finalmente (lastly)
- Frecuentemente (frequently)
- Hoy (today)
- Luego (then)
- Mañana (tomorrow)
- Nunca (never)
- Ocasionalmente (occasionally)
- Posteriormente (afterward)
- Primeramente (firstly)
- Rara vez (rarely)
- Siempre (always)
- Ultimamente (lately)
- Ya (already)

These adverbs provide information about the time and frequency in which action happens. So, you can use them any time you wish to provide further clarification on the matter you are discussing. Consider these examples:

- Siempre estudiamos inglés por la mañana. (We always study English in the morning.)
- Los niños juegan ocasionalmente. (The children occasionally play.)
- Ellas van al cine mañana. (They go to the movies tomorrow.)
- Estoy en una reunión ahora. (I am in a meeting now.)
- Vamos a comer después del trabajo. (We are going to eat after work.)

Please note that the position of adverbs changes in these examples. In general, adverbs of time will go at the beginning of the sentence when the subject is omitted, as in "Siempre estudiamos inglés por la mañana." In this case, "siempre" goes at the beginning.

When the subject is included, the adverb tends to occupy the end of the expression unless it is part of an adverbial phrase, such as "después del trabajo." In this situation, the adverbial phrase acts as one, long adverb.

There is also one other possibility: you could place the adverb or adverbial phrase at the beginning of the sentence, followed by a comma. For example: "Hoy por la mañana, temenos una reunion." (This morning, we have a meeting.) In this example, we can see how the adverbial phrase is placed at the beginning of the sentence in order to establish time.

Given the fact that the previous examples illustrate the way adverbs are placed in a sentence, we can list other adverbs based on their categorization.

Place	Manner	Number	Affirmation	Negation	Doubt
Aquí	Así	Mucho	Sí	No	Quizá
Ahí	Bien	Poco	Claro	Tampoco	Tal vez
Acá	Mal	Más	Bueno	Nada	Acaso
Cerca	Major	Menos	Por supuesto	Apenas	Posiblemente
Lejos	Peor	Bastante	Naturalmente	Jamás	Seguramente
En frente	Como	Nada	Obviamente	Nunca	Probablemente
Debajo	Cuidadosamente	Cuanto	Definitivamente	Ninguno	Potencialmente
A la par	exitosamente	tanto	también	Para nada	Específicamente

Table 10. Adverbs in Spanish

Based on this list, you can gain or provide as much information as you need in order to get the message across. Considering that the location of adverbs is fairly straightforward, you can begin to construct your own sentences quickly and effectively.

Prepositions

With regard to prepositions, you can use them in basically the exact same manner as you would in English. In Spanish, prepositions are intended to indicate the relationship among elements in a sentence. Without them, sentences would lack consistency and logic. As such, the use of prepositions becomes critical when constructing logical sentences.

Spanish prepositions also have clear uses; that is, you can clearly determine in which cases a preposition is to be used.

The following chart illustrates the various propositions used in the Spanish language.

Spanish	English	Definition	Examples
A	TO/AT	Used to indicate direction, time, direction, frequency, object, manner, imperative	Vamos **a** tu casa. Tenemos reunion **a las** 10. Estudiamos inglés **a diario**. ¡**A** comer!
ANTE	BEFORE/ABOVE	Used to indicate location, preference	Todos somos iguales **ante** la ley. **Ante** todo, me gusta la pizza.
BAJO	UNDER	Used to indicate location and manner	La hoja está bajo el libro. No puedo trabajar **bajo** estas circunstancias.
CON	WITH	Used to indicate accompaniment, manner	Juego fútbol **con** mis amigos. Prepara la comida **con** cuidado.
DE	OF/FROM	Used to indicate origin and belonging	Soy **de** los Estados Unidos. Éste es el control **de** la televisión.
DESDE	SINCE/FROM	Used to indicate time and location.	Estudio inglés **desde** hace tres años. Trabajo **desde** mi casa.
DURANTE	DURING/FOR	Used to indicate the duration of time	Él habla **durante** horas.
EN	IN	Used to indicate the physical location, manner, and time.	El dinero está **en** el banco. No hacemos esto **en** mucho tiempo. Terminamos el reporte **en** 5 minutos.
ENTRE	AMONG	Used to indicate location	Estamos **entre** amigos.
EXCEPTO	EXCEPT	Used to indicate exclusion	Todos van **excepto** yo.
HACIA	TOWARD	Used to indicate direction	Vamos **hacia** la oficina.

HASTA	UNTIL	Used to indicate duration	Trabajamos **hasta** la media noche.
MEDIANTE	BY	Used to indicate manner	Nos pagan **mediante** cheque.
PARA	FOR	Used to indicate reason	Esto es **para** ella.
POR	BY	Used to indicate direction, objective and time	Jugamos **por** mucho tiempo. Caminamos **por** la calle. Ellos trabajan **por** dinero.
SEGÚN	ACCORDING TO	Used to indicate manner	**Según** mi jefe, hoy es día libre.
SIN	WITHOUT	Used to indicate exclusion	No puedo ir **sin** mi teléfono.
SOBRE	ABOUT/ON	Used to indicate location, topic	El dinero está **sobre** la mesa. Estamos hablando **sobre** temas importantes.

Table 11. Prepositions in Spanish

The previous chart is rather comprehensive and provides you with a solid overview of the preposition structure in Spanish. So, it certainly pays to become familiar with the various types of prepositions and their use. It should be noted that they don't always translate directly from English to Spanish and vice-versa. Nevertheless, the chart above makes a great effort to simplify this understanding. That way, you won't have to guess the right meaning for each preposition. Instead, you will be able to make consistent sentences every time.

Conjunctions

Conjunctions function in a similar manner as prepositions. They join two parts of a sentence together as long as they have consistency and logic. This allows the speaker, or writer, to express a more complex idea in a single statement. Consequently, conjunctions act as a connector between two or perhaps more ideas.

The three conjunctions we will discuss are "pero" (but), "y" (and), and "o" (or).

"Y" (and) is used to indicate inclusion; that is, it is used to join two ideas together. For example, "me gusta comer pizza y beber refrescos" (I like to eat pizza and drink sodas). In this example, we are joining two ideas that are related to each other. This has logic and consistency since the sentence flows naturally.

Also, "y" can be used in a list of items. For instance, "necesitamos comprar pan, leche, huevos y cereal." (We need to buy bread, milk, eggs, and cereal.) Notice that we use "y" at the end of the list. As such, you can join both ideas and items by using "y."

A word of caution: It is common to see the liberal use of "y" in writing. This is actually an improper form as it creates run-on sentences. While it is not in line with writing best practices in Spanish, it is commonly done.

Consider this example:

- Vamos de vacaciones a Europa y vamos a visitar muchos lugares y luego vamos a comer comida deliciosa y queremos conocer lugares nuevos y es una experiencia bonita" (We are going on vacation to Europe, and we are going to visit many places, and then we are going to eat Delicious food and then we are going to know new places, and it is a great experience.)

To English speakers, the problem with this sentence is rather obvious. However, it is not quite the same with Spanish speakers. So, be on the lookout for this type of writing. The best way to go in this case is to write shorter sentences. Something like this would sound a lot clearer and organized:

- Vamos de vacacione a Europa. Vamos a visitar muchos lugares. Luego, vamos a comer comida deliciosa. Queremos conocer lugares nuevos. Es una experiencia bonita.

This organization is much easier to follow and understand as opposed to the first example we presented.

The next preposition is "pero" (but). This preposition indicates contrast. By "contrast," we mean a different idea or opinion of consideration. This conjunction helps maintain consistency, as it reflects logical ideas in a proper context.

Consider this example: "me gusta la pizza pero no me gustan los refrescos." (I like pizza, but I don't like sodas.)

In this example, the contrast occurs when you have a food you like, followed by one which you don't. These contrasting ideas warrant the use of "pero." Your sentences can be as simple or complex as need be. Maintaining consistency is a skill you need to accomplish. Otherwise, your sentence can get confusing.

Take another example: "me gusta la pizza y me gustan los refrescos, pero no me gustan las hamburguesas." (I like pizza, and I like sodas, but I don't like hamburgers.) In this example, you have introduced two conjunctions in the same sentence. You could tighten up this idea by saying, "me gusta la pizza y los refrescos, pero no las hamburguesas." (I like pizza and sodas but not hamburgers.) This second version will help make your writing much easier to follow.

The last conjunction is "o" (or). It is used to indicate an alternative. In this case, alternatives serve as choices or options that are presented. It is important to note that there could be more than two options, though you would have to structure your ideas accordingly.

For example:
- Podemos comer pizza o hamburguesas. (We can eat pizza or hamburgers.)
- Podemos comer pizza, hamburguesas o pollo frito. (We can eat pizza, hamburgers, or fried chicken.)

In the first example, there are two options. In the second, there are three. As such, you could have an infinite number of options, but only the last one presented ought to be preceded by the "o" conjunction. Actually, "o" works in much the same way that "y" does in a list of items.

One interesting orthographic rule is when "o" is used to separate numbers, it carries a tilde. For instance: "¿Es el número 50 ó 15? (Is the number 50 or 15?)

The reason for using a tilde is to avoid potential confusion between "o" and "0." While the RAE has indicated that this rule is no longer mandatory, it is still widely used, especially in older texts, to avoid potential confusion between the conjunction and any numbers.

If you are going to present phrases as alternatives, ensure that you keep the same consistency throughout your writing.

For example: "podemos ir al cine o podemos ir a comer." (We can go to the movies, or we can go eat.)

While it would also be valid to say, "podermos ir al cine or a comer." (We can go to the movies or eat.), the use of "podemos" (we can) makes a case for its inclusion in the second half of the sentence in order to maintain consistency.

Granted, many of these ideas and structures are applicable to writing; it should be noted that when having a conversation, you can get away with not following these structures, as long as you are able to get your idea across. Nevertheless, it pays to follow the proper structure so that you can avoid confusing your interlocutors.

Just like any other part of speech or grammar practice is the best way for you to hone your skills. So, do take the time to go over any of the items in this chapter in order for you to make the most of the materials presented. In the next chapters, we are going to be putting this knowledge to the test. Therefore, be ready to put your thinking cap on and create some interesting sentences so that you can express your ideas.

Chapter 16: Forming Sentences

Sentence formation in Spanish is quite similar to that in English. Spanish and English syntax are very similar despite several differences. We have spoken about these differences throughout this book. However, we are going to put them all together in this chapter.

First of all, the basic structure of a Spanish sentence is based on the "subject + verb + object" formula. This means that you can take this basic structure to build any sentence that you would like to construct. Let's see how we can build a sentence in the present simple.

- Yo juego fútbol todos los días. (I play soccer every day).

In this example, the subject is "yo" (I), the verb is "juego" (play, conjugated for the first person in present simple), and the object of the sentence, which is an adverbial phrase "todos los días" (every day).

Based on this example, you can see that building a sentence is rather straightforward. There aren't any complex rules that you need to follow in order to make sense of your ideas. As long as the verb is conjugated properly based on the tense you intend to use, you will be in good shape, moving forward. This is one important point to master.

Now, let us discuss one of the main differences between English and Spanish sentence formation.

Sentences Without Subject

Earlier, we talked about how it is possible to omit the subject of a sentence. In fact, it is quite common to do this, so long as it is clear about who or what you are referring to. If you omit the subject, but it is unclear who the person you are referring, then you might cause confusion in your interlocutor.

Consider this example:

- Trabajo en una oficina. (I work in an office).

The conjugation for "trabajo" makes it clear that you are referring to yourself. In this case, there is no question about who you are talking about. Hence, you can easily omit the subject because your interlocutor will be clear as to who you are referring to.

Please consider this example.

- Trabajo en una oficina. Mi hermano trabaja en un hospital. Mi mejor amiga trabaja desde casa. Es un buen trabajo. (I work in an office. My brother works in a hospital. My best friend works from home. It is a good job.)

This example makes reference to three people. While this is not the issue, the actual issue lies in the "es un buen trabajo" part of the paragraph. What job are you talking about? Whose job are you referring to?

If you base your assumptions on logic, you could infer that the job you are referring to is the last one mentioned; that is, your best friend's. However, if you are actually referring to your own job or that of your brother's, then you will quickly confuse your interlocutor.

Here is a clearer version:

- Trabajo en una oficina. Mi hermano trabaja en un hospital. Mi mejor amiga trabaja desde casa. Mi trabajo es bueno. (I work in an office. My brother works in a hospital. My best friend works from home. My job is good.)

As you can see, it is perfectly fine to refer to an earlier point in the paragraph. As long as you make this clear, you should have no worries about confusing your interlocutor. Nevertheless, be on the lookout in case the folks with whom you speak commit this error. While they may do it involuntarily, it may confuse you.

In that case, you can just seek clarification by using questions such as:

- ¿Cuál trabajo? (Which job?)
- ¿Tu trabajo o el de tu hermano?) (Your job or your brother's?)
- ¿El trabajo de quién? (Whose job?)

There is no need to feel embarrassed when asking for clarification. Spanish culture does not frown upon asking questions. In fact, asking for clarification can be used to show genuine interest in the conversation. So, don't be afraid to ask for more information if you are not clear on something being said.

Another important aspect of sentence formation is negatives.

Negative Sentences

Earlier, we mentioned the use of "no" in order to build negatives. This is the case, as Spanish does not use any special auxiliaries to build negative sentences. In fact, you can simply use "no" in a regular, affirmative statement, and you should be good to go. But, there is one catch: the use of "no" needs to be in the right spot.

Let us illustrate with a couple of sentences:

- Yo no trabajo en una oficina. (I don't work in an office.)
- Yo no estoy trabajando ahora. (I am not working now.)

In both of these examples, you can see that we are using "no," following the subject and preceding the verb. This is the correct placement of "no." If you happen to place it anywhere else, then it might lead to potential confusion.

In addition, you can omit the subject of the sentence. That would look something like this:

- No trabajo en una oficina. (I don't work in an office.)
- No estoy trabajando ahora. (I am not working now.)

In this case, "no" becomes the first word of the sentence as it is indicating the negation straight away. So, as long as you place "no" before the verb, you will be making a meaningful sentence.

When responding to questions, it is optional to use "no" at the beginning of your reply, or just jump right into the reply itself. Consider this question:

- ¿Quieres un café? (Do you want a coffee?)
    - No, gracias. (No, thank you).
    - No me gusta el café, gracias. (I don't like coffee, thank you.)
    - No tomo café, gracias. (I don't drink coffee, thank you.)

In these examples, you can simply reply using "no." This makes for a much simpler way of replying in the negative form.

One other important aspect of sentence formation in Spanish is the use of time expressions.

Time Expressions

You will find that Spanish speakers use time expressions, either at the beginning or the end of a sentence. This can be somewhat confusing, given the fact that English assigns a specific placement for time expressions. In essence, the placement of time expressions in Spanish depends on what the speaker is trying to get across. For example, the speaker might be more concerned about emphasizing the time expression itself. As such, that would warrant the speaker to place it at the beginning of the sentence. In other cases, the time expression itself might not be as important. So, that might motivate the speaker to place it at the end of the sentence.

Let's have a look at some examples.

- Hoy es mi cumpleaños. (Today is my birthday.)
- Mi cumpleaños es hoy. (My birthda is today.)
- Mañana trabajamos desde casa. (Tomorrow, we work from home.)
- Trabajamos desde casa mañana. (We work from home tomorrow.)
- Ella viaja la próxima semana. (She travels next week.)
- La próxima semana ella viaja. (Next week, she travels.)

In the above examples, you can see how the placement of the time expression can come at either the beginning or the end of the sentence. This illustrates how Spanish syntax is rather flexible. While there is a proper word order that needs to be followed, the main takeaway from this point is that even if you get the word order wrong, you should still be able to get meaning across.

So, don't worry too much about getting the exact word order right since Spanish gives you the opportunity to play around with the placement of words and adverbial phrases.

However, there is one caveat. When you use the subject and verb in a sentence, make sure you don't place them at different points. Consider this example:

- Nosotros mañana viajamos. (We tomorrow travel)

In this example, the time expression "mañana" was inserted in between the verb and the subject. This placement is incorrect. While the insertion of "no," as in, "nosotros no viajamos" makes sense, the use of the time expression would be incorrect. While it is still possible that your interlocutor will get the message, it would simply sound strange and

out of place. So, do take care to ensure that you don't insert time expressions in this location.

Overall, making sentences in Spanish is rather straightforward. The most complex part about it is getting the right verb conjugation. But with the guidelines we have presented in this book, you are well on your way go getting the right conjugations. As you gain more practice and experience, you will also be able to make the most of your language skills. As such, you will be able to construct solid sentences in no time.

Chapter 17: The Imperative and Subjunctive Moods

Indicative Mood

In general, Spanish speakers use the indicative mood when engaging in regular conversation. An indicative mood is a form used to provide information, state facts, and even express opinions in the past, present, future, and conditionals.

As such, the use of the indicative mood is the most commonly used form to express meaning. Thus far, we have focused on the indicative mood. The tenses that we have discussed are all centered on this mood.

Consider this example:

- Estoy viendo la televisión. (I am watching television.)

This example illustrates how you can express a fact. The fact in this example is that you are watching television.

This seems pretty straightforward, right?

Indeed, the indicative mood is the most commonly used mood in regular conversation. However, things change somewhat when you move away from the indicative mood and enter the subjunctive.

Subjunctive Mood

You probably have not heard of the subjunctive mood, as it is not a common topic in English classes. However, it is widely used in Spanish. In fact, the subjunctive is used about as much as the indicative mood. It is one of the nuances that native Spanish speakers develop more out of custom and habit than out of sheer linguistic proficiency.

You are probably wondering what the subjunctive mood is and how its use translates to the English language.

The subjunctive mood is essentially used to express wishes, obligation, necessity, desires, and doubt. Consequently, we are moving away from expressing facts and opinions to a bit of a gray area in which we are not necessarily talking about things that are clear-cut.

As such, the subjunctive is used any time you move away from "real" situations and into situations that reflect conditions, which are not always true at the moment. Hence, desires, wishes, and doubt fall perfectly into this category.

So, let us delve more into the expression of wishes and desires. In this case, you are referring to situations where you would like something to happen but may not necessarily have the ability to make it happen at the time of speaking or may seem unlikely at some point. You can even express situations that are completely unreal.

For instance, you might be thinking about situations where you wish you had millions of dollars or that you could change something that is impossible to change. These

circumstances, given the fact that you are not talking about a fact, would fall into the realm of the subjunctive.

Here are some expressions that generally accompany the subjunctive:

- Desear que (to wish that)
- Esperar que (to hope that)
- Exigir que (to demand that)
- Mandar que (to order that)
- Ordenar que (to order that)
- Pedir que (to ask that)
- Preferir que (to prefer that)
- Querer que (to want that)

Notice that we are talking about expressions that refer to things that you wish, hope, and prefer to happen. Also, you can see how there are actions that you can order or demand to be done. Now, it should be noted that these are not direct orders or requests. When you make a request using the subjunctive form, you are either requesting that something be done as a result of a condition being met, or you are simply trying to be much more polite about it.

The subjunctive can also be used to talk about emotions or reactions to certain situations. The underlying reason for the use of the subjunctive when expressing reactions and emotions is the use of the expression "es + adjective + que." This expression, when used to express emotions or reactions, is a signal that you are using the subjunctive form.

Here are some examples of this construction:

- Es absurdo que (it is absurd that)
- Es bonito que (it is nice that)
- Es Bueno que (it is good that)
- Es fundamental que (it is essential that)
- Es importante que (it is important that)
- Es inútil que (it is useless that)
- Es justo que (it is fair that)
- Es triste que (it is sad that)
- Es urgente que (it is urgent that)
- Me encanta que (I love that)
- Me gusta que (I like that)
- Me molesta que (it bothers me that)
- Me sorprende que (it surprises me that)

Notice how these constructions all represent ideas and feelings, which may not necessarily be true at the time of speaking. While you might be talking about something that is very much present at the time of speaking, you might also be talking about something that hasn't even happened yet.

Consider this example:

- Es importante llegar a tiempo. (It is important to get there on time.)

In this example, the subjunctive form in Spanish matches up quite well with the subjunctive form in English. While the use of the subjunctive in English isn't nearly as prevalent as it is in Spanish, the previous example makes a great case for using this form in both languages.

One other case in which the subjunctive is used is when the speaker is expressing doubt or disbelief. The following expressions are characteristic of this case.

- No creer que (not to believe that)
- Dudar que (doubt that)
- No opinar que (not to think that)
- No pensar que (not to think that)

You can also use the following conjunctions with the subjunctive mood.

- A fin de que (in order to)
- A menos que (unless)
- Antes de que (before that)
- Sin que (without)
- Con tal de que (provided that)
- Ojalá (hopefully)
- Quizá (maybe)
- Para que (so that)
- Tal vez (perhaps)

Below are words pertaining to time that can also be used:

- Cuando (when)
- En cuanto (as soon as)
- Hasta que (until)
- Después de que (after)
- Tan pronto como (as soon as)

As you can see, there is a good deal of expressions that signal the use of the subjunctive. As you gain more experience with the subjunctive, you will automatically begin to recognize what expression or part of speech prompts the subjunctive form usage. So, it certainly pays to do your homework.

Imperative Mood

The other mood used in Spanish is the imperative mood. In short, the imperative is used to give direct orders and commands. In English, the imperative allows the speaker to omit the use of the subject as it is implied that the subject of a command is "you." The same rule applies in Spanish.

Now, you might be wondering what differences there would be between the use of the imperative mood and commands given in the subjunctive. First of all, orders and requests given in the subjunctive can be directed at anyone. In the case of the imperative, the orders and commands given are directed specifically to "you."

As with the subjunctive, verb conjugation changes to reflect the difference in mood. Here is a general overview of such changes in conjugation.

With regular AR verbs, you can use the following rule of thumb.

- Verb: hablar (to speak)
    - (tú) habla – no hables (negative form)
    - (usted) hable
    - (nosotros) hablemos
    - (ustedes) hablen

Notice how the verb conjugation changes in the endings given to the verb. Also, the subject is placed in parentheses as it is not used when actually saying such phrases, but we have included them to illustrate the subject we are referring to.

The conjugation of the regular IR verbs, as well as ER verbs, can be viewed as follows:

- Verb: comer (to eat)
    - (tú) come / no comas (negative form)
    - (usted) coma
    - (nosotros) comamos
    - (ustedes) coman

Once again, you can see how the verb endings reflect a variation in the regular conjugation. As you become familiar with this form, you will notice how straightforward it actually is. The challenge, of course, is to recall the proper endings in this mood.

There are also irregular verbs that can be used in the imperative mood. So, here are the most common commands used:

- Di (say)
- Haz (do)
- Pon (put)
- Sal (come out)
- Sé (be)
- Ten (have)
- Ve (go)
- Ven (come here)

Consider these examples:

- Di algo (say something)
- Haz un esfuerzo (make an effort)
- Pon tu nombre (put your name)
- Sal a jugar (come out to play)
- Sé honesto (be honest)
- Ten paciencia (have patience)
- Ve a dormir (go to sleept)
- Ven conmigo (come here with me)

These examples all illustrate commands that you can express using the imperative mood. Also, they use the (tú) form. So, you can easily use them whenever you are asking your interlocutor to carry out an action at any given point.

Ultimately, the use of the indicative, subjunctive, and imperative all boils down to the situation where you find yourself communicating. Consequently, you can use any of these moods to get your message across effectively. So, do take the time to go over the various moods so that you can recognize them.

Chapter 18: Making Comparisons

The basic structure for the comparative form in Spanish is rather straightforward. As such, you can quickly begin to put it into practice in order to express your ideas.

In essence, comparisons boil down to the use of adjectives to compare two or more objects or people. This structure is evidenced by the "más + adjective + que" expression. This expression takes the adjective, which is the focal point of the comparison.

Comparative Form

It is important to keep in mind that this comparison is about two items. The adjective in question is meant to compare the two items that are contrasted. Virtually any adjective can be used in this case. So, let's consider some examples of this structure:

- Roberto es más alto que Diego. (Roberto is taller than Diego.)

In this example, we are using the verb "ser" since we are discussing permanent conditions. After all, height is a rather permanent condition that cannot be altered. Therefore, we generally use the verb "ser" to compare and contrast the characteristics of individual items. Next, we have "más" (more) and the adjective in question. "Alto" (tall) agrees in both gender and number. That means if the items in question are in singular form or plural, the adjective must reflect this difference. This is also the case if the items are feminine or masculine. Then, "que" introduces the second item in question.

Let's consider the following example to illustrate agreement in terms of both number and gender.

- Las niñas son más rápidas que los niños. (Girls are faster than boys.)

In this example, we are comparing two groups, that is, girls and boys. As such, "niñas" (girls) is plural. This means that the adjective "rápidas" (fast) must agree both in terms of number and gender. This is a key point to keep in mind as this is applicable to all cases. Nevertheless, we are still comparing two items, even if they are actually a number of items grouped into a single one.

Similarity

If you would like to indicate that two items are the same or not, you can use this expression: "igual que" (same as).

With this expression, you are indicating that two items are the same. For instance: "un libro digital es igual que un libro físico" (a digital book is the same as a physical book.) In this example, you are making clear that both items are the same; that is, there is no difference between them.

Now, consider this situation:

- "Un libro digital no es igual que un libro físico" (A digital book is not the same as a physical book.)

In this example, you are simply saying that both items are different. While you are not specifying where the difference lies, you are stating that the items in question do not have the same characteristics.

So, you can use this structure to simply make a point that two items or groups of items are the same or different. Ultimately, your use of this structure is intended to mark the difference or similarity between the items in question.

Superlative Form

When you are comparing more than two items, you can use the superlative form. This form indicates that there is one item that is "more" or "less" than the rest. This form can be used anytime you are comparing any number of items in excess of two.

Consider the following example:

- Alejandra es la mejor estudiante de quinto grado. (Alejandra is the best student of the 5th graders.)

In this example, you are saying that "Alejandra" is the best student out of all the students in Grade 5. While the number of students isn't known (at least from simply reading the statement), it is clear that "Alejandra" is the best one of all. This implies that there are at least three students in the class.

You can even use this form to refer to an immense number of objects. For instance:

- Los agujeros negros son los objetos más grandes del universo. (Black holes are the largest objects in the universe).

In this case, we are comparing the vast number of objects in the universe. So, given the fact that there is an unfathomable number of objects out there, it is a good idea to use the superlative form to make such a generalization.

Consequently, you can see that the main difference lies in the use of "el/la" or "los/las." This is what underscores the use of the superlative form. Consider this other example:

- El Ferrari es el auto más costoso. (The Ferrari is the most expensive)

In this example, you are making it clear that it is "the most expensive," thereby making proper use of the superlative form. However, keep in mind that this form needs to agree in both number and gender. So, "los agujeros negros" is masculine plural. By the same token, "el Ferrari" is masculine singular.

Of course, you could also make other types of generalizations that are intended to reflect an opinion. The example, "Laura es la chica más bella del mundo" (Laura is the most beautiful girl in the world) is intended to reflect a personal opinion more than anything else. As such, you can use this form to reflect your personal opinions and beliefs about a person or object.

In this case, we are making an agreement with a singular feminine noun, that is, "Laura." As you gain more practice with this form, you will be able to recognize quickly the difference that lies among the various nouns and their corresponding agreements.

Comparison of Verbs

One other use of the comparative and superlative forms lies in the comparison of verbs. Technically speaking, this comparison requires the use of adverbs since you would be describing an action. Nevertheless, the structure and use of adjectives remain the same.

Consider the following examples:

- Fernando juega fútbol mejor que Pablo. (Fernando plays soccer better than Pablo)
- Nancy habla más despacio que Patricia. (Nancy speaks slower than Patricia)
- Los niños comen menos que los adultos. (Kids eat less than adults)
- Los dólares valen más que los pesos. (Dollars are worth more than pesos)
- Las computadoras trabajan más eficientemente que las máquinas de escribir. (Computers work more efficiently than typewriters)

In these examples, we can see how the comparison among objects is focused on the way certain actions are done, as opposed to the characteristics of these items themselves. Consequently, you can use the same form, though instead of using the verb "ser," you can virtually use any verb that you wish to take into account.

Notice in the sentence, "Las computadoras trabajan más eficientemente que las máquinas de escribir," where we are using the adverb "eficientemente" (efficiently) to highlight the difference between the two items. Thus, you can virtually use any adjective or adverb to state your comparisons.

Also, keep in mind that all adjectives and adverbs are preceded by "más" (more) or "menos" (less). Hence, there is no need for transformations, such as "nice" into "nicer." This makes expressing comparisons much more straightforward as compared to English.

Chapter 19: Short Stories

In this chapter, we are presenting five short stories that you can read to practice the language which we have discussed throughout this book. Each story has its own topic, where important vocabulary is presented before the story. Then, you have the story, which you can read at your own leisure.

Once you have gotten through the story, you will find some questions about it. Each of the questions is intended to help you practice both reading comprehension and grammar skills. The responses to these questions are based on the text itself. Also, we have included suggested answers in order to provide you with some guidance.

So, do take the time to go over these questions; they will help you get the most out of the various topics, which we have covered in this volume. Furthermore, you can see the language in a real-life context. Indeed, this is a great combination.

Most importantly, you can begin to practice the language that we have discussed throughout this book in an engaging manner. As such, here is a suggested methodology that you can apply to the study of these short stories.

1. First, please review the vocabulary presented at the beginning of the story. The words in that vocabulary have been selected in order to help you warm up for the content in the story. You will find both the Spanish and English words in the list. That way, you won't have to guess their meaning. You can read through the list, and make a note of the words that you find new or challenging.
2. Next, read through the story, paragraph by paragraph. Since you will find the Spanish and English version, you will be able to visualize the structures and conjugations that we have studied throughout this volume. That way, you will be able to make a mental note of the way each structure is presented in real-life. This makes learning grammar and sentence structure a lot more digestible.
3. Then, go through every one of the paragraphs. When you reach the end of the story, go back to any parts that you feel weren't clear or perhaps you have questions about. You can focus on these parts so that you can get the extra practice that you need. Once you feel comfortable with the entire story, you can then move on to the questions.
4. The questions following the story are both meant to test your reading comprehension and give you an opportunity to practice your writing skills. This exercise will provide you with the chance to use your imagination as it pertains to writing skills.
5. Finally, the suggested responses at the end of the story are meant to serve as a guide. So, you can compare your own answers to the suggested ones. Of course, these are only suggested answers. That means you can very well come up with your own answers according to the passage that you have read.

We have some tips that will help you get the most out of these stories based on the methodology suggested:

- Don't feel that you need to get through the entire story in one session. In fact, each story has been designed so that you can take one paragraph at a time. Also, you can begin with the vocabulary and then take each paragraph as time allows you. That way, you won't feel like you have been interrupted. If anything, you will be able to pick up with where you left off.
- Take your time. There is no need to rush through the stories or any part of this book. This volume can very well serve you as a reference guide. That way, you can always go back to it whenever you have the need to do so.
- Try your best to set aside a specific amount of time each day for study with this book. Even 10 or 15 minutes a day is enough to get you into the habit of daily practice. Since practice is the best way in which you can improve your skills, you will soon find that getting into a groove is not nearly as hard as you thought it would be. So, do try to make some time during a break at work, your daily commute, or even before bedtime to go through parts of each story or any other part of this book. We are sure that you will not only find it enjoyable but also productive.

We hope you enjoy every one of these stories. They have been carefully crafted to provide you with practice and meaningful experience.

Story #1: Un nuevo empleo / A New Job

Vocabulario Importante	Important Vocabulary
contador	accountant
departamento	apartment
películas de acción	action movies
experiencia	experience
universidad	university
además	in addition
viajar	travel
sueño	dream
disciplina	discipline
comprar	buy
empleo	job
optimista	optimistic

Francisco es el nuevo **contador** de la empresa "La Mejor." Él es un chico joven. Tiene veintisiete años. Es de Nueva York y vive en un **departamento** con su perro Bruno. Francisco le gusta jugar fútbol y ver **películas de acción** en los fines de semana.

Francisco tiene cinco años de **experiencia**. Actualmente, está estudiando en la **universidad**. Está en el último año de su carrera. Francisco espera graduarse el próximo año. **Además**, tiene muchos planes para el futuro.

Primero, Francisco desea **viajar** por Europa. Este es un **sueño** para él. Francisco desea conocer París, Londres y Madrid. El segundo plan que tiene es comprar un coche nuevo. Él sabe que con su trabajo y un poco de **disciplina**, él puede comprar el coche que quiere. El tercer plan que tiene es **comprar** su propio departamento. Para esto, él necesita mucho dinero, pero está dedicado a lograrlo.

Francisco is the new **accountant** at the company "La Mejor." He is a young guy. He is twenty-seven years old. He is from New York and lives in an **apartment** with his dog, Bruno. Francisco likes to play soccer and watch **action movies** on the weekends.

Francisco has five years of **experience**. Currently, he is studying at the **university**. He is in the last year of his course of study. Francisco hopes to graduate next year. **In addition**, he has many plans for the future.

First, Francisco wants to **travel** to Europe. This is a **dream** for him. Francisco wants to know Paris, London, and Madrid. The second plan he has is to buy a new car. He knows that with his work and a little **discipline**, he can buy the car he wants. The third plan that he has is to **buy** his own apartment. To do this, he needs a lot of money, but he is dedicated to achieving it.

Hoy es el primer día de su nuevo **empleo**. Él está seguro de que es un buen trabajador y que sus resultados son buenos. Francisco está muy **optimista** del futuro que tiene en su nuevo puesto de trabajo. Le deseamos todo lo mejor a Francisco con sus planes.

Today is the first day of his new **job**. He is sure that he is a good worker and that his results are good. Francisco is very **optimistic** about the future that he has in his new job. We wish Francisco all the best with his plans.

Preguntas sobre la historia

¿Quién es Francisco?
_____
_____
_____

¿En qué empresa trabaja?
_____
_____
_____

¿Con quién vive Francisco?
_____
_____
_____

¿Qué desea Francisco?
_____
_____
_____

¿Qué quiere Francisco comprar?
_____
_____
_____

Questions about the story

Who is Francisco?
_____
_____
_____

In what company does he work?
_____
_____
_____

Who does Francisco live with?
_____
_____
_____

What does Francisco want?
_____
_____
_____

What does Francisco want to buy?
_____
_____
_____

Respuestas sugeridas	**Suggested responses**
¿Quién es Francisco?	Who is Francisco?
Es un chico joven de veintiocho años. Es contador en una empresa.	He is a young guy. He is twenty-eight years old. He works in a company.
¿En qué empresa trabaja?	In what company does he work?
Él trabaja en la empresa "La Mejor."	He works at the company "La Mejor."
¿Con quién vive Francisco?	Who does Francisco live with?
Francisco vive con su perro Bruno.	Francisco lives with his dog, Bruno.
¿Qué desea Francisco?	What does Francisco want?
Él desea viajar a Europa.	He wants to travel to Europe.
¿Qué quiere Francisco comprar?	What does Francisco want to buy?
Él quiere comprar un coche y un departamento nuevo.	He wants to buy a car and a new apartment.

Story #2: Como hacer nuevos amigos / How to Make New Friends

Vocabulario Importante	Important Vocabulary
oportunidad	opportunity
algunas	some
presentarte	introduce yourself
útiles	useful
también	also
conversación	conversation
consiste	involves
apropiadamente	appropriately
preguntas	questions
amable	kind
tímidas	shy
consejos	tips

Cuando conoces a una persona nueva, tienes una **oportunidad** de hacer un nuevo amigo. Por eso es que debes conocer **algunas** frases importantes que puedes utilizar para **presentarte** y conocer mejor a tu nuevo amigo.

Frases como, "¿cuál es tu nombre?" y "¿de dónde eres?" son muy **útiles** para conocer mejor a tus nuevos amigos. **También** puedes usar frases como, "mi nombre es _____" y "soy de _____." Con estas frases, puedes iniciar una buena **conversación**.

Una buena conversación **consiste** en hacer **preguntas** interesantes y responder **apropiadamente**. Si haces buenas preguntas y escuchas a tu nuevo amigo, es seguro que la conversación es positiva. De lo contrario, puede parecer aburrido. Por eso es muy importante ser amigable, atento y **amable**.

Las personas **tímidas** tienen problemas para hacer amigos algunas veces. Cuando te sientes nervioso al conocer a una persona nueva, simplemente debes

When you meet a new person, you have an **opportunity** to make a new friend. That's why you should know **some** important phrases that you can use to **introduce yourself** and get to know your new friend better.

Phrases like, "what's your name?" and "where are you from?" are very **useful** for getting to know your new friends better. You can **also** use phrases such as, "My name is _____" and "I am from _____." With these phrases, you can start a good **conversation**.

A good conversation **involves** asking interesting **questions** and answering them **appropriately**. If you ask good questions and listen to your new friend, it is certain that the conversation is positive. Otherwise, you may seem bored. That is why it is very important to be friendly, attentive, and kind.

Shy people have trouble making friends sometimes. When you feel nervous when meeting a new person, you should simply take a deep breath and greet the person

respirar profundo y saludar a la persona cordialmente. Una sonrisa también es una buena manera de iniciar una conversación. También es buena idea aprender el nombre de tu nuevo amigo. Siempre es buena idea llamar a las personas por su nombre. Así, les puedes mostrar que pones atención y estás interesado en conocerlos bien.

Con estos **consejos**, puedes hacer amigos rápidamente. No necesitas habilidades especiales. Solo necesitas ser una persona auténtica. De esa manera, siempre tienes una buena oportunidad para conocer nuevas personas y hacer amigos interesantes.

cordially. A smile is also a good way to start a conversation. It is also a good idea to learn the name of your new friend. It is always a good idea to call people by their name. Thus, you can show them that you pay attention and are interested in knowing them well.

With these **tips**, you can make friends quickly. You do not need special skills. You just need to be an authentic person. That way, you always have a good opportunity to meet new people and make interesting friends.

Preguntas sobre la historia

¿Qué debes hacer cuando conoces a una persona nueva?
_____
_____
_____

¿Cuáles frases puedes utilizar?
_____
_____
_____

¿En qué consiste una buena conversación?
_____
_____
_____

¿Qué es una buena idea cuando conoces a una persona nueva?
_____
_____
_____

¿Qué necesitas para hacer amigos??
_____

Questions about the story

What should you do when you meet a new person?
_____
_____
_____

What phrases can you use?
_____
_____
_____

What does a good conversation involve?
_____
_____
_____

What is a good idea when you meet a new person?
_____
_____
_____

What do you need to make new friends?
_____

Respuestas sugeridas	**Suggested responses**
¿Qué debes hacer cuando conoces a una persona nueva?	What should you do when you meet a new person?
Debe hacer preguntas interesantes sobre una persona nueva.	You should ask interesting questions about a new person.
¿Cuáles frases puedes utilizar?	What phrases can you use?
Puedes usar frases como "¿cuál es tu nombre?" y "¿de dónde eres?"	You can use phrases such as, "what's your name?" and "where are you from?"
¿En qué consiste una buena conversación?	What does a good conversation involve?
Una buena conversación consiste en poner atención a tu nuevo amigo.	A good conversation involves paying attention to your new friend.
¿Qué es una buena idea cuando conoces a una persona nueva?	What is a good idea when you meet a new person?
Es una buena idea recordar el nombre de tu nuevo amigo.	It is a good idea to remember your new friends' name.
¿Qué necesitas para hacer amigos?	What do you need to make new friends?
No necesitas nada especial, solo ser una persona auténtica.	You don't need anything special; just being an authentic person.

Story #3: Mi deporte favorito / My Favorite Sport

Vocabulario Importante	Important Vocabulary
activa	active
no puedo	can't
natación	swimming
especialmente	especially
usualmente	usually
después	after
gimnasio	gym
algunas veces	sometimes
tan bonito	such a nice
saludablemente	healthy
próximo	next
difícil	difficult

Soy una persona **activa**. Me gusta el ejercicio y los deportes. **No puedo** vivir sin hacer ejercicio y practicar deportes. Esto me hace sentir bien. Me siento motivada para trabajar y estudiar.

Mi deporte favorito es la **natación**. También me gusta correr y jugar tenis, pero la natación es mi deporte favorito. Disfruto mucho estar en el agua. El agua se siente excelente **especialmente** cuando hace mucho calor.

Voy a nadar tres veces por semana. **Usualmente** voy martes, jueves y sábado. Los demás días, voy al gimnasio **después** de mi trabajo. Tengo tiempo para ir una o dos horas al **gimnasio** los lunes y miércoles.

Algunas veces, tengo oportunidad de jugar tenis con mis amigos. Podemos jugar tenis los días domingo. El tenis es un deporte **tan bonito**. El tenis es más bonito que el fútbol. Es un gran ejercicio.

También me gusta comer **saludablemente**. Siempre hay verduras y frutas en mis comidas. También agrego

I'm an **active** person. I like exercising and sports. **I can't** live without exercising and playing sports. This makes me feel good. I feel motivated to work and study.

My favorite sport is **swimming**. I also like to run and play tennis, but swimming is my favorite sport. I really enjoy being in the water. The water feels excellent, **especially** when it is very hot.

I go swimming three times a week. I **usually** go on Tuesday, Thursday, and Saturday. On the other days of the week, I go to the gym **after** work. I have time to go, for an hour or two, to the **gym** on Mondays and Wednesdays.

Sometimes, I have the opportunity to play tennis with my friends. We can play tennis on Sunday. Tennis is **such a beautiful** sport. Tennis is more beautiful than football. It is a great exercise.

I also like to eat **healthy**. There are always veggies and fruits in my meals. I also add chicken and fish in any meal that I eat. I

pollo y pescado cuando cocino las comidas. Me importa mucho estar en forma y saludable. Una vida saludable es esencial para vivir felizmente.

El **próximo** mes espero viajar a los Estados Unidos. Hay muchas montañas para escalar. Este es un deporte que quiero intentar. Sé que es **difícil**, pero es un reto que deseo superar. Yo sé que con esfuerzo puedo hacer cualquier cosa.

Y tú, ¿cuál es tu deporte favorito?

care a lot about being fit and healthy. A healthy life is essential to living happily.

Next month, I hope to travel to the United States. There are many mountains to climb. This is a sport that I want to try. I know it's **difficult**, but it's a challenge that I want to overcome. I know that with effort, I can do anything.

And you, what is your favorite sport?

Preguntas sobre la historia

¿Cuál es mi deporte favorito?
_____
_____
_____

¿Cuándo es el mejor momento para hacer mi deporte favorito?
_____
_____
_____

¿Qué alimentos me gusta comer?
_____
_____
_____

¿En qué consiste mi dieta?
_____
_____
_____

¿Cuándo visito los Estados Unidos?
_____
_____
_____

Questions about the story

What is my favorite sport?
_____
_____
_____

When is the best time to do my favorite sport?
_____
_____
_____

What foods do I like eating?
_____
_____
_____

What does my diet involve?
_____
_____
_____

When do I visit the United States?
_____
_____
_____

Respuestas sugeridas	**Suggested responses**
¿Cuál es mi deporte favorito?	What is my favorite sport?
Mi deporte favorito es la natación.	My favorite sport is swimming.
¿Cuándo es el mejor momento para hacer mi deporte favorito?	When is the best time to do your favorite sport?
Disfruto nadar cuando hace mucho calor.	I enjoy swimming when it is very hot.
¿Qué alimentos me gusta comer?	What foods do I like eating?
Me gusta comer comidas saludables.	I like eating healthy meals.
¿En qué consiste mi dieta?	What does my diet involve?
Mi dieta consiste en comida saludable como frutas y vegetales.	My diet involves healthy food, like fruits and vegetables.
¿Cuándo visito los Estados Unidos?	When do I visit the United States?
Viajaré a los Estados Unidos el próximo mes.	I will travel next month to the United States.

Story #4: Comer en un restaurante / Eating in a Restaurant

Vocabulario Importante	Important Vocabulary
sirven	serve
prácticos	practical
dinero	money
comida rápida	fast food
de hecho	in fact
todos los días	every day
ingredientes	ingredients
ensaladas	salads
grasa	fat
alta calidad	high quality
ambiente	atmosphere
comida casera	homemade food

Los restaurantes **sirven** todo tipo de comidas. Algunos restaurantes sirven comida rápida como pizza, hamburguesas, y tacos. Estos restaurantes están por todas partes. Son **prácticos** y no tienes que gastar mucho **dinero** para comer bastantes.

Pero, la **comida rápida** no siempre es saludable. **De hecho**, la comida rápida puede ser muy mala para la salud. Por eso debes cuidar de no comer mucha comida rápida. Lo mejor es no comer este tipo de comida **todos los días**.

Otro tipo de restaurantes sirven comida más saludable. Estos restaurantes preparan la comida con **ingredientes** frescos y ofrecen menús para personas que quieren perder peso. Puedes comer **ensaladas**, frutas y comida preparada sin **grasa**. Esta es comida nutritiva pero deliciosa.

Luego, existen restaurantes que sirven comida de **alta calidad**. Pero, estos restaurantes también son caros. Los precios son elevados y el **ambiente** es

Restaurants **serve** all kinds of meals. Some restaurants serve fast food, such as pizza, hamburgers, and tacos. These restaurants are everywhere. They are **practical**, and you don't have to spend a lot of **money** to eat a lot.

But **fast food** is not always healthy. **In fact**, fast food can be very bad for your health. That is why you should take care not to eat too much fast food. It is best not to eat this type of food **every day**.

Other restaurants serve healthier food. These restaurants prepare food with fresh **ingredients** and offer menus for people who want to lose weight. You can eat **salads**, fruits, and food prepared without fat. This is nutritious but delicious food.

Then, there are restaurants that serve **high quality** food. But, these restaurants are also expensive. The prices are high, and the **atmosphere** is very good. In

muy bueno. En estos restaurantes, puedes probar comida de todo diferentes países del mundo.

Finalmente, existen restaurantes que sirven **comida casera**. Este tipo de comida es similar a la comida preparada en casa. Usualmente, es comida local, pero es muy buena. Este tipo de restaurantes son los favoritos de los turistas. No te puedes perder un restaurante de comida casera en tu próximo viaje.

these restaurants, you can try food from the different countries of the world.

Finally, there are restaurants that serve homemade food. This type of food is similar to food prepared at home. It is usually local food, but it is very good. These types of restaurants are the favorites of tourists. You cannot miss a restaurant that serves homemade food on your next trip.

Preguntas sobre la historia

¿Qué tipo de comida sirven los restaurantes de comida rápida?
_____
_____
_____

¿Cómo es la comida rápida?
_____
_____
_____

¿Qué ingredientes se usan en la comida saludable?
_____
_____
_____

¿Cómo son los restaurantes de alta calidad?
_____
_____
_____

¿Cómo es la comida casera?
_____
_____
_____

Questions about the story

What type of food do fast food restaurants serve?
_____
_____
_____

What is fast food like?
_____
_____
_____

What ingredients are used in healthy food?
_____
_____
_____

What are high-quality restaurants like?
_____
_____
_____

What is homemade food like?
_____
_____
_____

Respuesta sugeridas	**Suggested responses**
¿Qué tipo de comida sirven los restaurantes de comida rápida?	What type of food do fast food restaurants serve?
Los restaurantes de comida rápida sirven pizza, hamburguesas y tacos.	Fast food restaurants serve pizza, hamburgers, and tacos.
¿Cómo es la comida rápida?	What is fast food like?
La comida rápida es práctica, pero es mala para la salud.	Fast food is practical, but it is bad for your health.
¿Qué ingredientes se usan en la comida saludable?	What ingredients are used in healthy food?
La comida saludable usa ingredientes frescos.	Healthy food uses fresh ingredients.
¿Cómo son los restaurantes de alta calidad?	What are high quality restaurants like?
Los restaurantes de alta calidad son caros y el ambiente es muy bueno.	High quality restaurants are expensive, and the atmosphere is really good.
¿Cómo es la comida casera?	What is homemade food like?
La comida casera es como la comida preparada en casa.	Homemade food is like food prepared at home.

Story #5: De compras en el centro comercial / Shopping at the Mall

Vocabulario Importante	Important Vocabulary
edificio	building
tiendas	shops
entre otros	among others
encontrar	find
compras	shopping
estacionamiento	parking lot
vehículos	vehicles
clientes	customers
relacionadas	related
por ejemplo	for example
niños	children
seguramente	surely

Un centro comercial es un **edificio** en donde existen **tiendas** y restaurantes. Las tiendas son negocios donde hay productos que puedes comprar. Estos productos son ropa, zapatos, electrónicos, muebles, libros, **entre otros**.

Además, puedes **encontrar** restaurantes en un centro comercial. Estos restaurantes pueden ser de comida rápida, o de otro tipo de comida. Muchas personas van de **compras** y luego pasan a un restaurante a comer algo.

En un centro comercial, encuentras un **estacionamiento**. El estacionamiento es el lugar donde los **clientes** del centro comercial dejan sus **vehículos** mientras hacen compras o visitan un restaurante. Existen lugares marcados para cada coche. Normalmente, debes pagar una cantidad de dinero por el uso de estacionamiento.

Los días en donde más personas visitan los centros comerciales son sábado y domingo. Estos dos días son el fin de semana. Por lo regular, los fines de semana son para actividades que no están

A shopping mall is a **building** where there are shops and restaurants. Stores are businesses where there are products you can buy. These products are clothes, shoes, electronics, furniture, and books, among others.

In addition, you can **find** restaurants in a mall. These restaurants can be fast food or other kinds of food. Many people go **shopping** and then go to a restaurant to eat something.

In a mall, you can find a parking lot. The **parking lot** is the place where mall **customers** leave their **vehicles** while shopping or visiting a restaurant. There are marked places for each car. Normally, you must pay an amount of money for the use of the parking.

The days where more people visit the malls are on Saturday and Sunday. These two days are the weekend. Usually, weekends are for activities that are not work-**related**. **For example**, they are used to

relacionadas con el trabajo. **Por ejemplo**, se usan para pasar tiempo en familia. Existen muchas actividades en un centro comercial los fines de semana especialmente para **niños**.

Seguramente hay un centro comercial cerca de tu casa o tu trabajo. Puedes ir con tu familiar a disfrutar de un buen momento, comprar artículos a buenos precios, y salir de la rutina, al menos durante el fin de semana.

spend time with family. There are many activities in a shopping mall on weekends, especially for children.

Surely, there is a mall near your home or your place of work. You can go with your family to have a good time, buy items at good prices, and break your usual routine, at least during the weekend.

Preguntas sobre la historia

¿Qué es un centro comercial?
_____
_____
_____

¿Qué productos puedes comprar en un centro comercial?
_____
_____
_____

¿Qué es el estacionamiento?
_____
_____
_____

¿Qué días visitan los clientes el centro comercial?
_____
_____
_____

¿Qué puedes hacer en un centro comercial?
_____
_____
_____

Questions about the story

What is a shopping mall?
_____
_____
_____

What products can you buy in a shopping mall?
_____
_____
_____

What is the parking lot?
_____
_____
_____

What days do customers visit the shopping mall?
_____
_____
_____

What can you do at a shopping mall?
_____
_____
_____

Respuestas sugeridas	**Suggested responses**
¿Qué es un centro comercial?	What is a shopping mall?
Es un edificio con muchas tiendas y restaurantes.	It is a building with many shops and restaurants.
¿Qué productos puedes comprar en un centro comercial?	What products can you buy in a shopping mall?
Puedes comprar ropa, zapatos, electrónicos y libros entre otros.	You can buy clothes, shoes, electronics, and books among other
¿Qué es el estacionamiento?	What is the parking lot?
Es el lugar en donde los clientes estacionan sus vehículos.	It is the place where customers park their vehicles.
¿Qué días visitan los clientes el centro comercial?	What days do customers visit the shopping mall?
Los días que los clientes visitan el centro comercial son los sábado y domingo.	The days that customers visit the shopping mall are Saturday and Sunday.
¿Qué puedes hacer en un centro comercial?	What can you do at a shopping mall?
Puedes hacer las compras o comer en un restaurante.	You can do shopping or eat in a restaurant.

Conclusion

We are at the end of this journey into the world of Spanish. We are certain that you have learned much about the Spanish language, how it works, and how you can use it to your advantage. The most important thing is that you got through the entire book. This means that you are committed to learning Spanish.

Of course, learning a language is not easy. It takes time and dedication. Total mastery of language is a skill that is crafted over years of practice and experience. Nevertheless, we all need to start somewhere. If you never take that first step, you will never be able to attain a level of proficiency with which you are comfortable.

So, we would certainly encourage you to keep reviewing and practicing the content in this book. It has been designed in such a way that each time you go through a section or chapter, you will always find something new to think about. This is the type of exercise that will help you hone your skills and further develop your abilities.

At this point, what is the next step?

First of all, go back and review any parts that you feel were challenging or particularly interesting. By reviewing a part of this book, or even the entire volume itself, you will find that it will help you reinforce your understanding of each topic. This will then allow you to springboard into more advanced topics.

Next, be sure to take as many notes as you need to. Note-taking will help you to fixate language in your mind. In short, writing things down on paper is a great way to force your brain to take permanent note of the language you have learned. What this means is that you are exercising the various skills that are involved in the learning process. Consequently, you will get as much as you can out of this book.

Then, setting up a daily practice schedule will help you to build consistency and momentum in your learning. Often, we don't have much time to spare. Yet, there is always some way where you can spare 10 or 15 minutes a day. This could mean taking some time away from your lunchtime, using your commute, or even taking a few minutes before going to bed. It doesn't matter when you are able to make time. What does matter is that you do it. You will find that as you make more time to study, you will build a habit that will eventually lead you to become consistent in your progress. Before you know it, you will begin to see results.

Also, finding Spanish-speaking friends is a great way to test your new language skills. It is very likely that any Spanish-speaking friends that you might have will be more than willing to help you practice what you have learned in this book. Also, this type of practice and exposure will enable you to play with the language so that you can become comfortable with going off-script. This will allow you to truly begin to communicate through the use of what you have actually learned.

If you are planning on traveling, you will find that the language presented in this book will be invaluable as you navigate your way through the various places and situations that you will encounter. Best of all, you will have the opportunity to put yourself to the test.

There is an undeniable feeling of satisfaction that comes when you are able to communicate in a foreign language.

We are confident that you found the content in this book useful in any situation. In fact, don't be surprised if you get caught in learning Spanish. You might even choose to pursue your learning even further.

In that case, do check out the subsequent volumes in this series. You will find that they are intended to help you deepen your knowledge and understanding of the Spanish language in such a way that you will be truly on your way to mastering Spanish communication skills.

So, thank you for taking the time to read this book. There are plenty of options out there which claim to teach you Spanish in a short period of time. Unfortunately, some of those courses under-deliver in terms of value, while others turn out to be a costly experience.

If you have found this book useful and informative, do tell your friends, colleagues, and family members. Perhaps they have been looking for a viable alternative to learn Spanish. In that case, they will hopefully get as much out of this book as you have.

Thank you once again. See you in the next volume.